HOSANNA

A

take up & READ

PUBLICATION

the WORD among us® Press

Published by The Word Among Us Press
7115 Guilford Drive, Suite 100
Frederick, Maryland 21704
www.wau.org

24 23 22 21 20   1 2 3 4 5

ISBN: 978-1-59325-378-3

Nihil Obstat: The Reverend Michael Morgan, J.D., J.C.L.
                     Censor Librorum
                     November 1, 2019
Imprimatur: +Most Reverend Felipe J. Estevez, S.T.D.
                     Bishop of St. Augustine
                     November 1, 2019

Editorial Director: Elizabeth Foss
Copy Editor: Rosie Hill
Editorial Assistant: Emily DeArdo
Cover Art, Illustration & Design: Kristin Foss
Research & Development: Elizabeth Foss, Colleen Connell

take up & READ

C O M M U N I T Y

VISIT US
takeupandread.org

BE SOCIAL
Facebook @takeupandread
Instagram @takeupandread
Twitter @totakeupandread

SEND A NOTE
totakeupandread@gmail.com

CONNECT
#TakeUpAndRead
#HosannaStudy

Start.

I am about to do a new thing;
  now it springs forth, do you not perceive it?
I will make a way in the wilderness
  and rivers in the desert.

ISAIAH 43:19

START DATE	PLACE

I'M FEELING

- ○ happy
- ○ excited
- ○ joyful

- ○ anxious
- ○ upset
- ○ tired

- ○ annoyed
- ○ angry
- ○ sad

- ○ grateful
- ○ confused
- ○ calm

- ○ _____
- ○ _____
- ○ _____

Outside my window:

Pondering:

Giving thanks for:

Clothed in:

Listening to:

In my prayers:

My hope for Hosanna:

Before You Begin:

An Introduction to Lectio Divina

Together, as a community of faithful women, today at the beginning of Lent, we are ready for a spiritual springtime. We are ready for new life—for a spiritual renewal of our minds, hearts, and souls. We are embracing Lent as a season to change our hearts and prepare the soil of our souls for the risen Christ.

How? How will the tired soul living in the woman in the middle of winter-gray be energized by the beginning of a season of penance? How will she find hope and new energy in the hard work of repenting?

She will pray—more. That's right. She will take more time to pray even though so many things pull on her time. Can we do that together? Can we take up for ourselves the ancient tradition of *lectio divina* and let the Word lead us to live in charity? We can and we must. This is the best way to prepare ourselves for Easter with peaceful composure and serene grace.

In his 2010 apostolic exhortation *Verbum Domini*, Pope Benedict XVI beautifully instructs the faithful to prayerfully read the Scriptures. Following his lead, we will be drawn into a practice that is as old as

Scripture itself. We will closely read and ponder Scripture passages carefully chosen for this season.

In the early Christian communities, Scripture was read to nourish faith with the wisdom of truth. When we hold the New Testament, we take up the understanding that the first Christians had of the Old Testament, together with the divine revelation the Holy Spirit granted to Jesus' earliest followers.

The Church Fathers' faith was informed by their careful, prayerful reading of the word. Today, we are blessed to welcome their wisdom into our reading when we access the commentaries that were the fruit of their *lectio*. The monastic movement grew in the fertile soil of *lectio divina*. The daily, ordered life of the monks was (and is) centered upon spiritual reading of Scripture. Can ordinary women in the twenty-first century find spiritual nourishment and new life in this age-old practice of holy men and women?

We can.

There are five steps in the pattern—five distinct movements that will direct the way we travel through our days. First, we read. Then, a meditation engages the mind, and we use reason to search for knowledge in the message. The prayer is the movement of the heart toward God, a beseeching on behalf of the soul. The contemplation elevates the mind and suspends it in God's presence. Finally, the action is the way we live our lives as gift of charity toward others. It's a tall order, but it's the very best way to live.

Let's take a careful look at each step.

Pope Benedict writes, "It opens with the reading (*lectio*) of a text, which leads to a desire to understand its true content: *what does the biblical text say in itself?*" (*Verbum Domini*, 87). This is where we explore the literary genre of the text, the characters we meet in the story, and the objective meaning intended by the author. We usually offer several passages which work together towards a common theme. You can choose just one passage, or you can look at the group together, as the Holy Spirit inspires. A good study Bible and/or a Bible dictionary will help you to place the reading in context.

"Next comes meditation (*meditatio*), which asks: *what does the biblical text say to us?*" (*Verbum Domini, 87*). Prayerfully we ponder what personal message the text holds for each of us and what effect that message should have on our lives.

"Following this comes prayer (*oratio*), which asks the question: *what do we say to the Lord in response to his word?* Prayer, as petition, intercession, thanksgiving and praise, is the primary way by which the word transforms us" (*Verbum Domini, 87*). What do we say to God in response to his Word? We ask him what he desires of us. We ask him for the strength and grace to do his will. Moved by his mercy, we give him thanks and praise.

The fourth act is "contemplation (*contemplatio*), during which we take up, as a gift from God, his own way of seeing and judging reality, and ask ourselves *what conversion of mind, heart and life is the Lord asking of us?*" (*Verbum Domini*, 87). Here, we reflect on how God has conveyed his love for us in the day's Scripture. We recognize the beauty of his gifts and the goodness of his mercy and rest in that.

Let God light you from within and look out on the world in a new way because you have been transformed by the process of prayerful Scripture study.

Finally, the whole point of this time we've taken from our day is to get up from the reading and to live the gospel. *Actio* is where we make an act of our wills and resolve to bring the text to life in our lives. This is our fiat.

> The process of *lectio divina* is not concluded until it arrives at action (*actio*), which moves the believer to make his or her life a gift for others in charity.
>
> We find the supreme synthesis and fulfillment of this process in the Mother of God. For every member of the faithful Mary is the model of docile acceptance of God's word, for she "kept all these things, pondering them in her heart" (*Lk* 2:19; cf. 2:51). (*Verbum Domini*, 87)

Together, this Lent, we will endeavor to engage in *lectio divina* every day. To correlate with each day's Scripture passages, we've created pages both for your time of prayer and for your active time. We want this book to come alive in your hands, to bring you a spiritual springtime. Try to take the time each day to dig deep, but if you have to cut your time short, don't be discouraged. Ask the Blessed Mother to help you find pockets throughout the day to re-engage. You don't have to fill in every box. There is no right or wrong answer. And you don't have to dig deeply with every passage.

Pray the parts you can, and trust the Holy Spirit to water the Word in your soul. Know that God can do loaves and fishes miracles with your small parcels of time, if only you are willing to offer him what you have. Before Lent gets swallowed with the ordinary to-do lists of seasonal hustle, sit in prayer and see how you can tune your heart to the beat of the Lord's heart, and ensure that the best gift you give this season is your life, given for others in charity.

Introduction

For this season, we will consider together the Gospel of Matthew. Even if we had the whole year—even if we had a lifetime—the treasure that is Matthew's Gospel is inexhaustible. We could meditate upon it every day and never run out of good news.

The early church was comprised of the people who walked with Christ, ate with him, witnessed his life, and prayed with their voices joined with his. After his death, this community grew into a life of prayer, and practice, and preaching. The Gospels of Matthew, Mark, Luke, and John

> *are the primary devotional, meditational reading to deepen our faith as Christians. They are the place where we meet Christ. Saint Teresa of Avila said she never found anything as powerful as the Gospels for growing in holiness, even the deepest writings of the greatest saints and mystics.* (Peter Kreeft, *You Can Understand the Gospels and the Book of Acts, 181)*

St.Matthew wrote his Gospel for his fellow Jews. He wanted to share with them the good news of the fulfillment of the prophecies of the Savior. We see lots of references to the Old Testament throughout the Gospel of Matthew, as he weaves in the Scripture the Jews would have known in order to point them to how Christ meets them in the promises of their heritage. Matthew, a tax collector for the Roman government, would have been despised by his fellow Jews and would have been a most unlikely convert. But in the upside down kingdom of Christ, the unlikely happened, and Matthew was an eyewitness to the Word, and he then faithfully gave to us a written account of the good news of the kingdom.

This is a challenging Gospel. In the Sermon on the Mount, Jesus offers the highest of moral standards and then he goes further: his followers are called not only to follow the law but to change their hearts. He asks us to do what we can't, what is so difficult it is beyond human capability.

Then, he gives us himself.

The moral law is not our salvation. Christ is. God infuses us with supernatural grace. Peter Kreeft writes,

> *Many modern readers dislike Matthew's Gospel because of its hard sayings, its warnings against riches and worldliness, its announcement of divine justice and judgment, and its demand for good works. If we dislike this book, then this is precisely the book we need most. For we need to know the whole Gospel. It is precisely those aspects of it that we still find repellent and try to avoid that we need most—not those we already understand and love.*

Lent stretches out before us—a long season, an opportunity to dig deeply into this Gospel, to embrace its difficult passages, and to journey towards the resurrection. The Word will change us. He is living and breathing and he wants so much to have our whole hearts and to give us his whole heart. Let this be a season of that holy exchange. Let it be a season of good news.

We're praying for you.

Elizabeth Foss
Founder and Chief Content Director
Take Up & Read

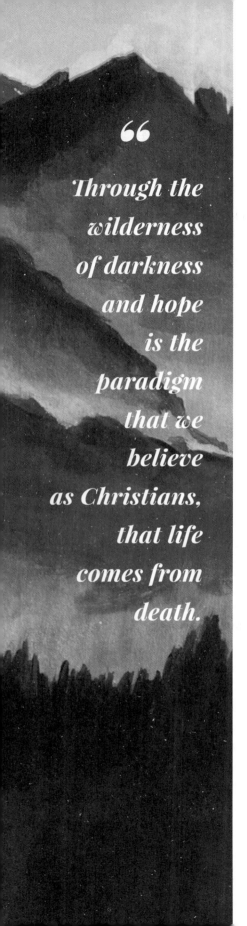

> **Through the wilderness of darkness and hope is the paradigm that we believe as Christians, that life comes from death.**

When designing this book, I began looking for photos of the mountains in Galilee, pulling from the internet, with the Sermon on the Mount on my mind.

I took tones from the serene valleys, the sandy hills, and the pink sky to paint a mountain scene that shows contrast between the misery in darkness and the hope in light. As we study the Book of Matthew this Lent, keep this visual of contrast in mind as we climb a mountain together.

Through the wilderness of darkness and hope is the paradigm that we believe as Christians, that life comes from death. We are promised a bright kingdom through the beatitudes and the gospel, if we are up to doing the work.

This book's design is meant to feel like a handbook, a wilderness guide to lead you through Matthew and to help you spiritually thrive throughout Lent.

We used clean headings in this book to minimize distractions. The arrows and vertical margins are to help organize both your head and heart on the Scriptures. The Lectio Divina journaling page is clean and spacious so you can write out how you encounter the word, but we took special care to break down the beatitudes in a different format. We designed an opportunity to "check in" on Selah days, to keep your Lent going strong, and a few small extras that will help to enhance your Scripture study.

I'm learning what our faith means through the Bible, alongside you.

Kristin Foss
Designer of *Hosanna*

intentional design

We want to connect you with the word, so we take special care to make each of our studies unique and intentionally designed. In this Scripture study, we explore the Gospel of Matthew, with a focus on God's mercy. We have added tools to help you break down the beatitudes, with a special journaling layout to help you examine how to live out what God is asking of you.

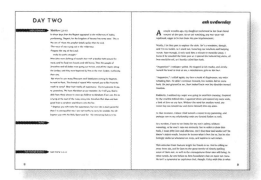

DAILY READINGS

Each day we will focus on a reading from the Gospel of Matthew. Further readings are listed for you to continue your study and make more connections with the Bible.

LECTIO DIVINA

Reflect upon the word with this simple journaling tool. Meditate or answer directly onto the page.

SELAH

Here is a chance to pause for prayer, praise, and rest.

We added check-ins on Selah days to leisurely check in on your heart and well-being.

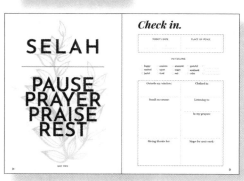

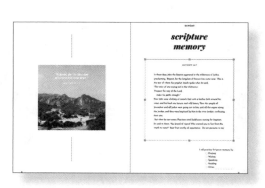

WEEKLY SCRIPTURE VERSE

We will memorize one key verse of the beatitudes to reflect upon each week. By the end of this study, you will know them inside out.

BEGIN

week of ash wednesday

ASH WEDNESDAY

OPEN YOUR BIBLE

Matthew 4:23

Jesus went throughout Galilee, teaching in their synagogues and proclaiming the good news of the kingdom and curing every disease and every sickness among the people.

NOTES

FOR FURTHER READING

MATTHEW 9:35
MATTHEW 1:1-17
MATTHEW 2:13-18

LECTIO DIVINA

hosanna

What is Jesus saying or doing in this passage?

What does this passage reveal to me about God's mercy?

In what area of my life do I need to hear this message of mercy?

ash wednesday

In today's Scripture, we find a tidy summary of Jesus' ministry while he was on the earth. "Jesus went throughout Galilee, teaching in their synagogues and proclaiming the good news of the kingdom and curing every disease and every sickness among the people" (Matthew 4:23). Jesus' purpose on earth was to preach the ways of the kingdom of God, ensuring that the people understood how they were called to conduct their lives. Then, he told them why they should behave that way; he shared the good news and helped them to understand the glory of the kingdom as best they could on this side of heaven. Finally, he demonstrated the power of God. He calmed the storms, cast out the demons, and healed the sick.

Lent asks us to return to this triad of preaching and gospel and miracle again and again. Sometimes, I begin Lent with the intent to clean all the things. I'm going to examine my conscience and confess my sins and clean out the pantry and donate half the contents of my closet to a worthy cause. I'm going to super clean, and when I get to Easter, I will shine with splendid brilliance and so will everything around me. Usually, I crash and burn around the third week of Lent.

It's not just that my frenzied physical cleaning is not sustainable over forty days; it's that I've overlooked the third component of the triad. St. Matthew carefully delineates the rules of Christian life, and he shares why Christians want to live within the ethics of the kingdom of God. Then, he spends a great deal of time showing how God overcomes the natural to infuse the Christian world with the supernatural. And that's what we need to know in order to make this Lent a good one. We need to know our sins and to repent of our sins, but we also need to know how to grant mercy, and most of all, how to make ourselves available to God's mercy.

We will fall short of the holiness of the beatitudes. We will never fully attain the glory of the Sermon on the Mount during this lifetime. We will stumble over the same sins time and time again. And we might despair of ever breaking free of the bondage of sin in order to live the freedom of his good plan. It is here, in our lack, that we meet the hinge of the gospel. We don't have to break free of bondage in our own power. But we do have to recognize the hold of sin, and we do have to repent of giving our assent to its power. Then we have to ask for the supernatural power that breaks the bonds and sets us free.

This Lent, sit at the feet of Jesus on a mountain by the Sea of Galilee and listen as he shares what it is to live well. Take to heart his admonitions and examine your own life in their light, then see how he calls you to follow him down from that mountain, to do the work that waits for you among the people God puts in your path. Follow him down from the mountain and see how he heals the hurting and binds the wounded. Know that his healing is for you too. He can overcome the struggle and the pain. He can make all things truly shiny and new—even you. Especially you.

Elizabeth Foss

THURSDAY AFTER ASH WEDNESDAY

OPEN YOUR BIBLE Matthew 3:1-12

In those days John the Baptist appeared in the wilderness of Judea, proclaiming, "Repent, for the kingdom of heaven has come near." This is the one of whom the prophet Isaiah spoke when he said,

"The voice of one crying out in the wilderness:

'Prepare the way of the Lord,

make his paths straight.'"

Now John wore clothing of camel's hair with a leather belt around his waist, and his food was locusts and wild honey. Then the people of Jerusalem and all Judea were going out to him, and all the region along the Jordan, and they were baptized by him in the river Jordan, confessing their sins.

But when he saw many Pharisees and Sadducees coming for baptism, he said to them, "You brood of vipers! Who warned you to flee from the wrath to come? Bear fruit worthy of repentance. Do not presume to say to yourselves, 'We have Abraham as our ancestor'; for I tell you, God is able from these stones to raise up children to Abraham. Even now the ax is lying at the root of the trees; every tree therefore that does not bear good fruit is cut down and thrown into the fire.

"I baptize you with water for repentance, but one who is more powerful than I is coming after me; I am not worthy to carry his sandals. He will baptize you with the Holy Spirit and fire. His winnowing fork is in his hand, and he will clear his threshing floor and will gather his wheat into the granary; but the chaff he will burn with unquenchable fire."

NOTES

FOR FURTHER READING MATTHEW 3:13-17

LECTIO DIVINA

hosanna

What is John the Baptist saying or doing in this passage, particularly about Jesus?

What does this passage reveal to me about God's mercy?

In what area of my life do I need to hear this message of mercy?

thursday after ash wednesday

Repentance has always been a bit of a dicey topic for me. I don't take well to someone else preaching repentance to me. I feel things so deeply that often those words burrow so far into me that rather than becoming an exhortation to renewed hope in Christ, they become a festering wound of shame, completely defeating the purpose of the process. And left to my own devices, I will mentally charm and cajole myself into thinking that sin is a minor matter and mercy is great, and so let's just sweep all that pain under the rug and move on with happy faces. I write an alternative narrative for myself about sin and mercy—a narrative that is precisely counter to the real purpose of repentance.

Repentance calls out to me like a parched and dry desert for my soul—a spiritual place of mean conditions to be avoided, either because I will dive so far into the idea of deserving the punishing climate that I will give up and wither willingly, or because I will find ways to wear the appearance of sun-kissed skin and dry lips and look lovely while doing it.

John the Baptist, I've always thought, was the voice of those who call me into the wilderness, wanting me to sit in the desert of shame without regard for whether I will ever recover from what I experience there. And yet here he is in the Gospels, calling to me across the millennia; and there on those pages are the faithful ones who responded, coming to him from across the miles, eager to confess their sins and to be baptized by him.

Those faithful ones don't go out into wilderness to stay. They go, they confess their sinfulness, and they are baptized with water and admonished to "prepare the way of the Lord" (Matthew 3:3). They do not stay until shame has withered their hearts and parched their souls. They walk in long enough to feel their thirst for something better, for something more than they can be or have on their own. They spit out the dryness of their sin in a confession, and John quenches their hearts' thirst with the water of baptism and the promise of mercy coming.

During the process of my recent divorce, I found myself in the confessional on Good Friday, sobbing to the point that I am sure the words I spoke were mostly incoherent. I wish I could tell you that I left with my fears relieved and feeling refreshed and renewed by sacramental grace. But the truth is, I didn't. I left feeling judged and misunderstood, my throat burning with the taste of my tears and a new bitterness. A few weeks later, seated on a couch in the rectory across from my pastor, I spent more than two hours pouring out my heart story, talking and talking as he sat and listened, and listened more. The bitterness poured out alongside the self-doubt, the confusion, the pain, and the deep need to know that I was okay, and that God was okay with me.

When I stopped talking and forced my eyes upward to his face, he spoke words of assurance and hope. He had walked silently beside me into the desert, the wilderness of my tired and pained heart, and then he took my hand and walked me back out, the burning in my throat soothed.

The call to "prepare the way of the Lord" (Matthew 3:3) rings with a new sound when I reflect on that experience. It is a call of invitation—a road map winding not *to* the wilderness but *through* the wilderness, where what awaits is not a treacherous trap but a gentle hand cupping the water I need to quench my thirst and keep me going. Then I can walk out the other side of that wilderness and find myself on the banks of the great river of mercy flowing from Jesus' heart to my own.

We do not have to fear stepping into the wilderness because we do not embrace a faith that calls us to live there. The wilderness is only part of the journey—the place where we slough off the dryness of our sin, and we make our way to the River of Life. The call to repentance is a call to refresh our hearts so we are able to keep walking, recognize our thirst, and delight in the relief of a Savior whose heart bursts with life-giving water sprung from his great love for us.

Colleen Connell

FRIDAY AFTER ASH WEDNESDAY

OPEN YOUR BIBLE Matthew 4:1-11

Then Jesus was led up by the Spirit into the wilderness to be tempted by the devil. He fasted forty days and forty nights, and afterwards he was famished. The tempter came and said to him, "If you are the Son of God, command these stones to become loaves of bread." But he answered, "It is written,

'One does not live by bread alone,
but by every word that comes from the mouth of God.'"

Then the devil took him to the holy city and placed him on the pinnacle of the temple, saying to him, "If you are the Son of God, throw yourself down; for it is written,

'He will command his angels concerning you,'
and 'On their hands they will bear you up,
so that you will not dash your foot against a stone.'"

Jesus said to him, "Again it is written, 'Do not put the Lord your God to the test.'"

Again, the devil took him to a very high mountain and showed him all the kingdoms of the world and their splendor; and he said to him, "All these I will give you, if you will fall down and worship me." Jesus said to him, "Away with you, Satan! for it is written,

'Worship the Lord your God,
and serve only him.'"

Then the devil left him, and suddenly angels came and waited on him.

NOTES

FOR FURTHER READING MATTHEW 4:12-17

LECTIO DIVINA

hosanna
What is Jesus saying or doing in this passage?

What does this passage reveal to me about God's mercy?

In what area of my life do I need to hear this message of mercy?

friday after ash wednesday

Once I was visiting a friend in Savannah and trying to make it to Mass. While walking toward the cathedral, the sky turned a steely, dark gray. Powerful gusts of winds whipped through my hair and tugged at my clothing. I found myself conflicted. I thought I might be close to the church, but I wasn't positive and it could be dangerous roaming unfamiliar streets in a storm without so much as an umbrella. Hail began to pelt me, so my friend and I retreated into a cafe.

"That's the devil working to keep you from Jesus," my friend remarked.

My first reaction was to scoff at her. As if the devil comes in the form of sudden thunderstorms. Isn't that a little melodramatic?

Yet when the sky cleared with surprising alacrity revealing sunshine, I found myself thanking God. To show my gratitude, I decided to try to make it to Mass on time. I had just a few minutes to spare, so I sprinted off in the direction of the cathedral. As I ran through Savannah's streets, trying to not trip on patches of cobblestone, I realized my friend's words must have influenced me because in my mind I was talking to none other than the devil himself, saying, "You're not going to keep me from Mass."

Jesus' temptation in the desert teaches us many things: how the Son always trusted the Father; how temptations are many, but being tempted doesn't equate to rejecting God or sinning; and yes, that the devil is very real indeed and will do everything in his power to distract Christians from building God's kingdom—including, perhaps, giving us excuses to skip Mass.

God works in mysterious ways, but so does the devil. C. S. Lewis reminds us in *The Screwtape Letters* that remaining incognito is all part of the devil's plan. He works undercover so we won't recognize him. He wants to be about as believable as Freddy Krueger. Because if I'm not aware of him or his motives, or if I doubt he's a real presence in my life, then how can I possibly be on guard against him?

The devil doesn't tempt me as the proverbial red-faced demon, prodding me with a pitchfork to join the dark side. Nor have I had a personal taste of true evil, although I see glimpses of it in the news in statistics on genocide, abortion, and violence every day, as well as in the abuse scandals of my beloved Church.

In my own life, the devil disguises himself as rationalizations and my own self-doubt and lack of trust in God's plan. "I'm too tired to get everyone ready for Mass." "I can't speak at that event. I'm not qualified enough." "If I spend more money or lose more weight, this void in my heart will be filled." "This pregnancy wasn't a part of my plan. How will I ever handle another baby?"

That just may be the devil talking.

But every time I can shut out those nagging voices in my head, every time I refuse the poisoned apples the devil continues to tempt me with just as he did Eve—the lies that tell me I'm not good enough and need this worldly thing to be happier, or that I don't need Mass or God to figure things out—I draw closer to God.

The devil is real, but so is Jesus. Christ is present in every trial, struggle, and temptation, and like the angels ministered to him after his forty days of fasting and overcoming temptation, he will care for us. He is our strength. He will be there to pick us up when we fall. Jesus tenderly holds you close, and through prayer and sacrifice, he will help you during your Lenten journey and beyond, leading you ever closer to his kingdom.

Kate Wicker

SELAH

PAUSE PRAYER PRAISE REST

Selah is a Hebrew word found often in the psalms and a few times in Habakkuk. Scholars aren't absolutely certain what it means. It seems to be a musical or liturgical note—maybe a pause or maybe a crescendo.

We have set aside this day for you to use as your *selah*. Perhaps you pause here and just review what you have pondered thus far. Perhaps you rejoice here and use this space for shouts of praise. Or maybe you take the opportunity to fill in some gaps in the pages before this one.

It's your space. Give it meaning.

He said to them,
"Come away to a deserted place
all by yourselves and rest a while."
For many were coming and going,
and they had no leisure even to eat.

Mark 6:31

Check in.

TODAY'S DATE	PLACE OF PEACE:
_____ | _____	_____

I'M FEELING

- ○ happy
- ○ excited
- ○ joyful
- ○ anxious
- ○ upset
- ○ tired
- ○ annoyed
- ○ angry
- ○ sad
- ○ grateful
- ○ confused
- ○ calm
- ○ _____
- ○ _____
- ○

Outside my window:

Working on my heart:

Small successes:

Listening to:

In my prayers:

Giving thanks for:

Hope for next week:

"*Blessed are those who mourn, for they will be comforted.*"

MATTHEW 5:4

scripture memory

MATTHEW 5:3-4

"Blessed are the poor in spirit,
for theirs is the kingdom of heaven.

Blessed are those who mourn,
for they will be comforted."

I will practice Scripture memory by:
○ Praying
○ Writing
○ Speaking
○ Reading
○ Other: _____

VICES

Pride
self-promotion; selfishness; lack of understanding of our dependence on God; ungratefulness

Greed
being a slave to work in order to acquire material goods; trusting in stockpiles of money over God's providence; inordinate love of temporal things

Envy
resenting the happiness, excellence, or success of someone else; a sense of deprivation over a perceived lack in one's own life; comparison and competition that robs us of joy

Wrath
wanting harm for another; impatience with the shortcomings of another to the point of anger; bulldozing past the place of understanding

Sloth
stubbornly resisting God's will; refusing the joy that comes from God; fearing the change that comes with answering God's call; preferring worldly comforts over pursuing Christ with zeal; boredom that is a symptom of emptiness of soul; joyless workaholism that avoids the peace of Christ

Lust
escaping a numb soul in temporary carnal pleasure; dividing a soul against itself as it replaces genuine love with a cheap substitute

Gluttony
inordinate consumption of pleasure; the false notion that we can be happy by filling emptiness with worldly things

VIRTUES + **BEATITUDES**

Humility | The Poor in Spirit
selflessness; gratitude; trust in God

The Beatitudes

Over the next eight journal days we will study the beatitudes by breaking down the promises Jesus has made and defining the characteristics of each one through Scripture.

Use this chart to make connections between vices, virtues, and beatitudes.

Generosity | The Merciful
sharing one's goods and one's time and talents; trusting the Lord for provision; keeping a Sabbath rest; caring for one's body and soul; caring for others' bodies and souls

---

Charity | The Mourners
compassion that allows us to enter into the sorrows of another person and to mourn with them; tenderness for the sufferings of others, rejoicing in someone else's gladness; kindness

---

Patience | The Meek + The Peacemakers
a peaceful response towards another's failings; meekness; an understanding of one's own smallness before God; a desire to understand others

---

Magnanimity | The Hungry for Righteousness
desiring holiness above all else; living for others; having confidence that God will fill our souls with what we need to serve generously; diligence

---

Chastity | The Pure in Heart
moral wholeness; purity of heart; making a pure gift of oneself; desiring God wholly

---

Self-control | The Peacemakers and The Persecuted
moderation; bearing deprivation and persecution with holiness and peacefulness; sacrificing one's own will for the good of another

MONDAY OF THE FIRST WEEK OF LENT

OPEN YOUR BIBLE

Matthew 5:1-3

When Jesus saw the crowds, he went up the mountain; and after he sat down, his disciples came to him. Then he began to speak, and taught them, saying: "Blessed are the poor in spirit, for theirs is the kingdom of heaven."

NOTES

FOR FURTHER READING

GENESIS 18:27; 32:10
EXODUS 3:11; 4:10
JOB 42:5-6
ISAIAH 6:5
PSALM 51:17
MATTHEW 5:13

THEIRS IS THE KINGDOM OF HEAVEN

A PROMISE OF LOVE

Blessed are
the poor in spirit,
for theirs is
the kingdom of heaven.

THE BEATITUDE

THE ETERNAL VALUE

What does it mean to be poor in spirit?	What kind of transformation of the inner person is being asked of you by this beatitude?	Define the characteristics of HUMILITY

The beatitudes present a way of life that promises salvation and peace in the midst of the trials and tribulations on earth. How can you live this beatitude here and now?

Refer to the chart on pages 32 and 33 for more info on how to interpret the beatitudes.

BLESSED ARE THE POOR IN SPIRIT

monday of the first week of lent

There were six tabs open on my computer, each one representing an assignment, task, or dimension of my vocation. One was forms to be filled for a child's doctor's appointment. One was a writing assignment with a Bible tab open next to it. One was the costuming list for my girls' dance production with costumes I'd yet to sew highlighted in ballet pink. One was a grocery list. And then there was the tab with the household tasks needing to be accomplished before selling our home. The last one was the gut-punch tab because it was a list of all the maintenance things I hadn't done in the past few years.

I opened the laptop and instantly felt overwhelmed and insufficient. To be honest, this is not an alien feeling. I frequently feel as if I'm not up to the task, even on days when only one tab is open. There are days when I wonder at the number of children I have, the diversity of their needs, the sheer number of socks that need to be matched, and I don't know how I can possibly be a good mom that day. Some days I wonder how I can even be an adequate mom. Add the other callings—to be a wife, a writer, a small business owner, a nutritionist, and a chef—and my impulse is to burrow under the covers and stay there, admitting defeat before the day is even begun. And then there are the evenings, the darkness enveloping the mental list of things not yet finished or things not done well.

The reality is that I am helpless, and that is exactly where God wants me to be. The culture tells me that the antidote to my sense of insufficiency or guilt is to build my self-esteem and to build a treasury of measurable things of this world. But Jesus tells me otherwise. He tells me that to be poor in spirit—very much aware of how little and unworthy I am—is a blessing. We are all poor. We are all absolutely nothing without God. But some of us are poor in spirit; we are aware that we are helpless on our own and we are in need of the sovereign grace of God. That awareness is the blessing. Knowing we need God is the key that opens the door to doing his will on earth and to living with him forever in heaven. If we know we are nothing without him, then we frequently approach the throne of grace and ask to be empowered by the Holy Spirit.

Sometimes, we fall into a pull-yourself-up-by-the-bootstraps trap. We think if we just organize our time better, connect with the right people, and try harder, we'll be able to be as blissfully productive and serenely holy as our highest aspirations. The truth is that we need to acknowledge that we are not God and that thinking we can do it all under our own power is a sin—it stands in the way of grace. Acknowledging our need—recognizing our failures and our helplessness—allows us to be honest with Jesus and to beg him to come into our inadequacy and to equip us with his grace for his purposes. When we detach from the riches of this world—from all its material measures of success—then we are truly free. We are no longer enslaved to our desire for worldly things. Embracing the lifestyle of the poor in spirit, we're really living the life he intends for us. Then, we're really getting it done.

Elizabeth Foss

TUESDAY OF THE FIRST WEEK OF LENT

OPEN YOUR BIBLE Matthew 5:4

"Blessed are those who
mourn, for they
will be comforted."

NOTES

FOR FURTHER READING MATTHEW 5:14-16

FOR THEY WILL BE COMFORTED

A PROMISE OF LOVE

Blessed are those who mourn, for they will be comforted.

THE BEATITUDE

THE ETERNAL VALUE

What does it mean to be a mourner?	What kind of transformation of the inner person is being asked of you by this beatitude?	Define the characteristics of **CHARITY**

The beatitudes present a way of life that promises salvation and peace in the midst of the trials and tribulations on earth. How can you live this beatitude here and now?

Refer to the chart on pages 32 and 33 for more info on how to interpret the beatitudes.

BLESSED ARE THOSE WHO MOURN

a promise of love

tuesday of the first week of lent

It took three decades of the same argument over and over again (with different details each time) before I recognized the pattern. I'm not proud of this slow understanding, but I am encouraged by an intimate knowledge gained over time. It was so easy for me to see my husband's pattern when we argue, to think I knew what his goals were every time, but it took a very long time to recognize what I wanted every time. Why did I keep repeating the same pattern of argument and what could that pattern teach me about myself?

We've worked hard to know what we do now. Since I've long subscribed to the idea that wives would do well to sing their husbands' praises publicly and keep the rest to private conversation, we won't talk about his arguing style; we'll focus on mine. I am almost always seeking reassurance. I want to know that he is a safe person, that ours is a solid relationship, and that we are a couple that is healthy and whole. In the midst of an argument, I almost always want to be comforted.

For me, to be in conflict is to mourn. Peter Kreeft writes, "Mourning is the expression of inner discontent, of the gap between desire and satisfaction, that is, of suffering" (*Happiness: The First Three Beatitudes*). When I open the definition of mourning to this interpretation and I consider my intense need for reassurance, I see what Christ intended when he promised that those who mourn will be comforted.

He promised reassurance. He is the reassurance. He is the deep certainty, the safest of safe people, the most solid of all relationships, and the the truest expression of wholeness. The Father sent his Son into our suffering—all of our suffering—in order to satisfy our deepest needs for intimacy, understanding, and reassurance. He promised that our suffering has redemptive value.

Jesus is with us when we weep. He's there when we mourn in the most conventional use of the word, but he's also there in the many struggles of our everyday lives. Certainly, he is also there when it all becomes too much to bear and we despair. Jesus came to earth to sit with us as we open a bill for which there are no resources, as we answer a call that brings terrible news, and as we lie seemingly alone on a medical gurney. God knows what it feels like to be rejected, and to be betrayed. He knows the grief of broken relationships and prodigal children. Knowing all, he entered in. Every pain we suffer, he suffers too.

He was wounded when he walked the earth, and we wound him even now. But he doesn't turn away. Though we cause him pain, he stays. He reassures. His presence comforts us in a way nothing or no one on earth can. Even more astounding, he endures our sins. He is steadfast when we are not. We turn away from him over and over again with every sin, big and small, and he stays.

Emmanuel. God with us.

The Redeemer of our suffering comforts us in the sorrow. When life is crushingly hard, it is the Jesus of the scourging who absorbs the blows for us. He pours himself into us and we are strengthened. With that strength born of suffering, we have strength to offer others. He is risen and we are his body here on earth, blessed and broken for others. So, we stay. We enter into the sorrow. We offer ourselves.

We reassure a hurting world that there is hope.

His name is Jesus.

Elizabeth Foss

OPEN YOUR BIBLE ▶ Matthew 5:5

"Blessed are the meek,
for they will inherit
the earth."

NOTES ▶

FOR FURTHER READING ▶ MATTHEW 5:17-20

FOR THEY WILL INHERIT THE EARTH

A PROMISE OF LOVE

Blessed are
the meek,
for they will
inherit the earth.

THE BEATITUDE

THE ETERNAL VALUE

What does it mean to be meek?	What kind of transformation of the inner person is being asked of you by this beatitude?	Define the characteristics of **PATIENCE**

The beatitudes present a way of life that promises salvation and peace in the midst of the trials and tribulations on earth. How can you live this beatitude here and now?

Refer to the chart on pages 32 and 33 for more info on how to interpret the beatitudes.

BLESSED ARE THE MEEK

a promise of love

Until recently, my teenage daughter Katie was a fervent admirer of an Instagram "star" who grew up in our hometown. The star seemed to have it all—a beautiful home, a handsome and successful husband, a new baby, and a carefully cultivated feed that exuded peace and loveliness. She knew how to photograph and edit, how to work the algorithm, and how to display herself in order to be known. And since Katie followed her so closely, she was sure she knew this young woman very well. Then, one night, at an extended family dinner, my sister-in-law mentioned the Instagram star's husband, who was the son of a good friend. In the space of three sentences, everything Katie thought she knew proved itself to be untrue, and the mirage dissolved. Within the week, marriage was edited out of the Instagram feed, a divorce was announced, and the illusion was exposed for what it was.

While we don't all aspire to be internet stars, we all want to be known. We want to be understood and appreciated and recognized. And sometimes, we go to outrageous lengths to satisfy that longing. We create icons of ourselves, completely missing the fact that we are made in the image and likeness of a Creator whose time on earth was a witness to meekness—to being hidden and ignored. Jesus came as a baby and was born in a stable. He lived simply, spending the first thirty-three years of his life in obscurity and then moving out to fulfill his mission with quiet humility. He lived to do the will of his Father and to show us that this is the reason we live. God calls us to this meekness.

The meek who will inherit the earth are unconcerned with making themselves famous. Instead, meekness means that we want to know God and to understand what he desires of us. Meek people are not weak people; they aren't anxious shrinking violets. Meek people are very confident; their confidence is in the power of God and the quiet assurance that God is for them and not against them.

With such confidence, they are able to trust God and commit their lives to him. Instead of questing to be known, they understand that God knows them intimately and loves them unconditionally. There's no reason to edit oneself in order to acquire fans. Instead, the meek woman stands confidently before God, warts and all, and surrenders her faults to him, seeking God to redeem her. She doesn't pretend to be perfect. She acknowledges her imperfections and she acknowledges that Jesus is the only one who can perfect her.

In an age where Photoshop can fix a flaw in a second or two and a click can order up what one desires and have it on its way, a meek woman knows how to wait. She is patient and still in the presence of the Lord, and she trusts in his timing. She is steady in the storm that is a society in constant motion. While it might sound daunting, doesn't that steady trust sound very much like a blessing as well? Can we lay down our desires to impress and control, and instead be confident in God's perfect will and his perfect love?

Jesus doesn't promise that there won't be bumps in the road. He knows that even women who confidently trust in the Lord will encounter wicked people. It happens. He tells us exactly what to do.

> Be still before the LORD, and wait patiently for him;
> > do not fret over those who prosper in their way,
> > over those who carry out evil devices.
>
> Refrain from anger, and forsake wrath.
> > Do not fret—it leads only to evil.
> For the wicked shall be cut off,
> > but those who wait for the LORD shall inherit the land.
> (Psalm 37:7–9)

There is blessed, precious freedom in meekness. With peaceful detachment from worry and anger, the meek trust in the God who wants nothing but their good. How good it is to a live a life where we can endeavor to do his will and to wait patiently in cooperation with his plan! Meekness is authenticity in its truest sense. We know who we are, how we were created, and who empowers us to live the vision of our creation to its fruition. This life is a life of genuine strength and abundant inheritance.

Elizabeth Foss

THURSDAY OF THE FIRST WEEK OF LENT

OPEN YOUR BIBLE Matthew 5:6

"Blessed are those who

hunger and thirst

for righteousness,

for they will be filled."

NOTES

FOR FURTHER READING MATTHEW 5:29-30

FOR THEY WILL BE FILLED

A PROMISE OF LOVE

Blessed are those who hunger and thirst for righteouness, for they will be filled.

THE BEATITUDE

THE ETERNAL VALUE

What does it mean to hunger and thirst for righteousness?	What kind of transformation of the inner person is being asked of you by this beatitude?	Define the characteristics of **MAGNANIMITY**

The beatitudes present a way of life that promises salvation and peace in the midst of the trials and tribulations on earth. How can you live this beatitude here and now?

* Refer to the chart on pages 32 and 33 for more info on how to interpret the beatitudes.

BLESSED ARE THOSE WHO HUNGER AND THIRST FOR RIGHTEOUNESS

a promise of love

On New Year's Day, my ten-year-old burst into the kitchen in a flurry of excitement. She had her new planner in one hand and a box of markers and stickers in another. The day had come at last! It would have been remarkable to witness such glee over a new planner in a girl so young, except that I remember feeling exactly that way about a calendar when I was ten, and her older sisters and I were already deep into our own planners when she joined us. It's what we do: we look forward with great anticipation.

In the first four beatitudes, Jesus describes the emptying of oneself upon which the Christian life is founded: the littleness and hiddenness, the sorrow, and the quiet confidence that hungers for righteousness. The next four will offer us a picture of a merciful, pure peacemaker who will be persecuted for righteousness. The first three of these beatitudes show us how to lay down our lives for the Lord and how to be the vessel into which he can pour himself. In that emptiness, we know as St. Augustine did that "You have made us for yourself, and our heart is restless until it rests in you" (*Confessions*, 3). It is righteousness that fills us with God when we empty ourselves of anything and everything that is not God.

That human restlessness is God calling us to himself. He wants us to feel the need for him, and we do. Those planning pages lay empty before us and we have a deep, even urgent sense that we want to fill them with meaning and abundance. We all want to live lives of contented fullness. We have hungry hearts and souls; we scroll the internet or drive through the next neighborhood over, and we want what we don't have. Comparing and competing, we torment ourselves with the notion that there is always something more beautiful (and more blessed) just around the corner. God is calling in our insatiable longing, and all too often, we turn the other way. We waste hours on Netflix or shopping or gazing into other people's edited version of the elusive good life, thinking that somehow that's what we want to attain. And instead of being filled with goodness and mercy, we taste the bitterness of boredom, guilt, and loneliness.

Jesus tells us that there is blessing in recognizing our emptiness with an honest awareness—even grief—and there is blessing in accepting that we are nothing without him instead of trying to justify our brokenness or defend our lack. Once we acknowledge the emptiness for the promise it holds, we can see that hungering for righteousness is the path to blessed abundance. A peek ahead tells us we will be overflowing with mercy and peace.

What does this mean for the ordinary woman who holds this book on her lap and a cup of tea in her hands? What does it mean for the person whose planning squares fill with meetings and appointments and carpool commitments and soccer practices and dress rehearsals? It means God is calling you right where you are. You don't have to build a yurt near Walden Pond or cloister yourself away. You can fill with righteousness the ordinary everyday of late winter in your own hometown. You can be the woman who earnestly desires the grace to be a merciful, pure peacemaker in the midst of the crazy, chaotic existence that is our fallen world.

You are hungry and thirsty and restless and weary! Just stop. Today. Right now. Stop.

Make righteousness your passion. Hunger and thirst for acts of mercy. Look again at all those things you think you want, and all the places you compare yourself and come up short. This time, though, look through the lens of righteousness. Let God's perfect plan for merciful peace be the measuring stick. See how you can devote yourself to pursuing that plan and to be the instrument of that plan. As surely as you will eat and drink today, pursue what fills the soul—emptiness. Do justice, love kindness, walk humbly. Pursue purity and peace—in your soul, in your relationships, and in your own place in the world.

Elizabeth Foss

OPEN YOUR BIBLE

Matthew 5:7

"Blessed are the merciful, for they will receive mercy."

Corporal Works of Mercy

Feed the hungry
Give drink to the thirsty
Shelter the homeless
Visit the prisoners
Visit the sick
Bury the dead
Give alms to the poor

Spiritual Works of Mercy

Pray for the living
and the dead
Forgive injuries
Bear wrongs patiently
Comfort the sorrowful
Admonish the sinner
Counsel the doubtful
Instruct the ignorant

NOTES

FOR FURTHER READING   MATTHEW 5:33-37

FOR THEY WILL RECEIVE MERCY

A PROMISE OF LOVE

Blessed are
the merciful,
for they will
receive mercy.

THE BEATITUDE

THE ETERNAL VALUE

What does it mean to be merciful?	What kind of transformation of the inner person is being asked of you by this beatitude?	Define the characteristics of GENEROSITY

The beatitudes present a way of life that promises salvation and peace in the midst of the trials and tribulations on earth. How can you live this beatitude here and now?

* Refer to the chart on pages 32 and 33 for more info on how to interpret the beatitudes.

BLESSED ARE THE MERCIFUL

a promise of love

friday of the first week of lent

I have a confession to make: Twitter makes me crazy. I appreciate it as a gathering place, a virtual water cooler, and a forum for better understanding what people are thinking beyond the four walls of my home. But seriously, it makes me nuts. I have an incredibly low tolerance for snark; Twitter is all about snark. I cannot stand arguing for argument's sake; people on Twitter thrive on just such arguments. And I'm really, really bothered by people who profess to be progressive, enlightened, and tolerant but spend their days (and their tweets) touting their moral superiority. Then there is the perpetual refresh of the latest variation of bad news. Basically, I think Twitter is a hot mess.

I limit my time there. I carefully curate my feed. I try (sometimes successfully) to refrain from retorting. But recently, I've come to see Twitter as a mission field for mercy. What Twitter really needs is a big dose of mercy. And honestly, it's what our society is crying out for. Twitter is a reflection of the worst of us, and if I can be merciful on Twitter, I can extend that mercy beyond a screen and be a part of a movement for Christ that reflects the best of us.

Mercy begins in humility. The merciful person, instead of trying to one-up the next guy, sees clearly that without God she is nothing; she is spiritually bankrupt. The merciful woman is one who moves into her day—every day—grieving her sins and waiting with meekness for the Lord to satisfy her needs. In this posture of humility, she is open to God's blessing of mercy. Recognizing her brokenness, she knows that he is the Great Physician and that only he can heal. Mercy begets mercy. She is merciful to others because God is merciful to her.

The merciful person is not the person who is winning the argument on the internet or beating the other guy to the parking spot or touting moral superiority. The merciful person is the broken person. A woman is able to show mercy when she understands that she owes her entire being to Divine Mercy. To be merciful, we have to be ever mindful that life itself—and everything it encompasses—is the undeserved gift from a merciful God.

How will we greet the Lord when we meet him? Will we have a list of good works of mercy to show him, hoping to earn his mercy by an accounting of our deeds? That's not the way this works. Mercy isn't earned. Ever. By its very definition, mercy is undeserved.

And it's costly.

I cannot forgive your debt without paying it myself. One of us will be poorer in the transaction. And so, again, we hear the paradox of the kingdom. Christ assures us that extending mercy makes us rich in blessings. But God goes further. I can forgive your debt, but Jesus forgives the debt and then moves into the supernatural. He can forgive sin and remove it altogether. How can we be anything but humbled in the light of that glory?

I don't think that God is going to look at the balance sheet of mercy and make a judgment on our souls, trading our merciful deeds for his merciful eternity. Instead, he's going to look at our hearts. He's going to judge whether or not we surrendered to him with lowliness and meekness and then, drawing strength from the truth of his word and grace from the reality of his sacrament, whether we extended tender mercy to the people in our lives who are most undeserving, but also most wounded.

Perhaps, in this new world of constant contentious competition, mercy looks like seeking understanding instead of striving to prove a point. Perhaps it means seeing the wound whose stench is snark and sarcasm—and then binding that wound. Or maybe it's just as simple as conceding the prime parking space, smiling kindly at the person who gets it, and enjoying the walk a little further from the door.

A merciful woman stands outside of rapid-fire repartee. She looks around, absorbing detail and noticing needs. She stops on the way, kneels beside the injured, and recognizes God. She is not too important, too superior, or too busy to care and to serve. A merciful woman is a humble servant who fills with God and pours out his mercy generously for others.

Again, mercy begets mercy. Receive the Lord's mercy today, and see where the opportunities are to offer it others.

Elizabeth Foss

SELAH

PAUSE
PRAYER
PRAISE
REST

But you, beloved, build yourselves up on your most holy faith;
pray in the Holy Spirit; keep yourselves in the love of God; look forward to
the mercy of our Lord Jesus Christ that leads to eternal life.

Jude 20-21

Check in.

TODAY'S DATE	PLACE OF PEACE:
___	___	___	_____

I'M FEELING

○ happy ○ anxious ○ annoyed ○ grateful ○ _____
○ excited ○ upset ○ angry ○ confused ○ _____
○ joyful ○ tired ○ sad ○ calm ○ _____

Outside my window:

Small successes:

Giving thanks for:

Working on my heart:

Listening to:

In my prayers:

Hope for next week:

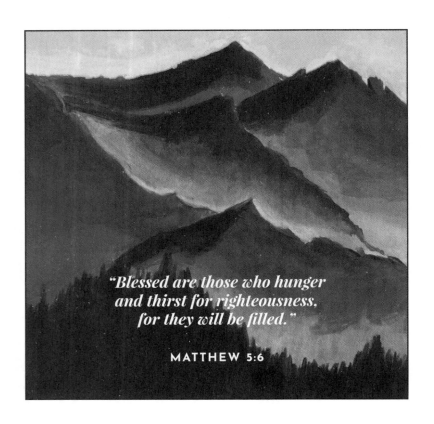

"Blessed are those who hunger and thirst for righteousness, for they will be filled."

MATTHEW 5:6

scripture memory

MATTHEW 5:5-6

"Blessed are the meek,

for they will inherit the earth.

Blessed are those who hunger and thirst for righteousness,

for they will be filled."

I will practice Scripture memory by:

○ Praying

○ Writing

○ Speaking

○ Reading

○ Other: _____

OPEN YOUR BIBLE

Matthew 5:8

"Blessed are the pure in heart, for they will see God."

NOTES

FOR FURTHER READING

MATTHEW 16:13-20
MATTHEW 5:38-39

FOR THEY WILL SEE GOD

A PROMISE OF LOVE

Blessed are
the pure in heart,
for they will
see God.

THE BEATITUDE

THE ETERNAL VALUE

What does it mean to be pure in heart?	What kind of transformation of the inner person is being asked of you by this beatitude?	Define the charateristics of CHASTITY

The beatitudes present a way of life that promises salvation and peace in the midst of the trials and tribulations on earth. How can you live this beatitude here and now?

Refer to the chart on pages 32 and 33 for more info on how to interpret the beatitudes.

BLESSED ARE THE PURE IN HEART

a promise of love

She didn't see me in the doorway, watching with my breath held. Little finger around the bottom of the cake, gathering sweetness as it moved, and then into her mouth, evidence disappearing in one delicious swallow. I waited a moment or two and then made my presence known. Offering a chance to make things right, right away, I exclaimed with feigned surprise, "Oh dear, what happened here? This cake has had a finger through the frosting."

"I don't know," said she, eyes wide and a telltale flush giving her away, even if I hadn't witnessed the crime.

I sighed. We were in for a struggle now. I've raised nine children and I'm still surprised the first time a child who seems so innocent—so pure of heart—proves that none of us is fully pure of heart.

Blessed are the pure in heart, for they will see God.

The people listening to Jesus as he spoke these words were probably a little confused. They knew Scripture. Throughout the Old Testament, the Jews were cautioned that no one can see the face of God and live. But Jesus tells them that if they are pure of heart, they can see the face of God. But then, one wonders whether, if she is a good Jew, does that mean she'll die?

To know God is to bear the mark of his love. That is what it is to be Christian: to love God and to be marked by his love. To live that love out in the world. The purest heart loves completely.

None of us can love Jesus as fully as he deserves. Frankly, none of us loves the people in our circle as fully as we should. We simply do not have pure hearts in a world riddled by impurities. If the four-year-old on a stool in my kitchen struggles with temptation, how much harder is it for the adult, out in the world, tempted daily by the forces of evil in a pitched battle for souls?

The recurring key to beginning to understand the beatitudes is that everything good in this world is a gift. God gives us purity of heart.

And he gives it to the undeserving. He gave it to Peter. When Jesus asked him who he thought he was, Peter was able to see with a pure heart that he was beholding the face of God. And Christ affirmed that the purity upon which he drew in order to recognize God was a gift. He told Peter that he had not perceived the divine through his senses; God himself had told him.

In that moment of recognition, Peter was given the grace of a pure heart—a heart that sees the face of God. But then even Peter, to whom so much has been given, could not continue to love unceasingly with a pure heart. He faltered and failed and sinned egregiously. Of course, God knew Peter would fail even after being given the grace to see Jesus for who he was. Still, Peter was the rock upon which the Church was founded. He was the one entrusted with the preservation and propagation of the good news after Christ was gone. Jesus recognized that Peter was humble and that Peter was open to grace. God knew that, with humility, grace would be enough.

Would I recognize God if he were standing in front of me, asking me who he is? It is an unlikely scenario, to be sure.

Would I recognize Christ if he were standing on a stool in my kitchen, destroying a birthday cake? Would I recognize him if he were gossiping about me with my neighbor? Would I recognize him if he hurt my child? Can I see Christ in the most unlovable of his creatures and, seeing him, can I love him with a pure heart? Or does my own sin stand in the way?

When confronted with my transgressions, do I lie to myself and to God, protecting my pride and hiding from the truth of impurities? Peter agonized over his choice to deny God and he fell humbly before the throne of mercy. God used him to love his Church.

My heart is not pure. Your heart is not pure. But God can make it so. He can fill your heart with grace. And when he does, you can extend that grace to an ever-widening circle of people to love.

Elizabeth Foss

Matthew 5:9

"Blessed are the peacemakers, for they will be called children of God."

MATTHEW 10:34-39
LUKE 12:49-53

THEY WILL BE CALLED CHILDREN OF GOD

A PROMISE OF LOVE

Blessed are
the peacemakers,
for they will be
called children of God.

THE BEATITUDE

THE ETERNAL VALUE

What does it mean to be a peacemaker?	What kind of transformation of the inner person is being asked of you by this beatitude?	Define the characteristics of PEACEFULNESS

The beatitudes present a way of life that promises salvation and peace in the midst of the trials and tribulations on earth. How can you live this beatitude here and now?

Refer to the chart on pages 32 and 33 for more info on how to interpret the beatitudes.

BLESSED ARE THE PEACEMAKERS

a promise of love

I'm a peacemaker through and through.

Or am I?

Here's the thing. I want peace. I want it all the time. I'm a person who cannot stand conflict. I'm the one always vigilant to see who might be unhappy, tripping over myself to make them happy. I want peace. I'm a peacemaker.

Except I'm not. Not really. Not in the sense of the beatitudes.

Jesus didn't come to remove conflict from our lives; he didn't come to create sweetness and light. He came to bring a sword (see Matthew 10:34). He came to set brother against brother (see Luke 12:49-53). We can't be saved without being changed, and peace comes when Jesus' sword excises our hardness and replaces it with his goodness. Even our most foundational human bonds are made new when we become the children of God.

All of salvation history, culminating in the great Easter story, is God's plan for peace between the humankind who rebelled and the God who loves us and wants us for himself. We are the daughters of the good Father and because we can take on his character and we can pursue peace the way that Jesus did. We are at war with evil itself. Imbued with the nature of our Father, we can be peacemakers after his own heart.

Peace isn't necessarily the absence of an argument or quiet instead of the exchange of ideas. Arriving at a place of peace is likely to involve some sacrifice, some discomfort, and maybe even some pain.

Peace comes with reconciliation. So, for each of us personally, peace necessarily begins with confession. We lay down our sins at the throne of mercy and exchange them for his forgiveness and actual grace. So changed, we become a force for peace in the world.

Making peace is about all the acts of love we can offer to overcome the distance between the good in ourselves and the good in other people. In every person is the spark of the divine. Peacemaking catches the spark and lights a fire of love.

For someone like me, who would rather avoid conflict at all costs, the peacemaking effort might be the difficult conversation that pushes past disagreement to understanding. On my own, I want to ignore or avoid someone who is contrary. Filled with the grace of our Lord, acting on the impulse of the Holy Spirit, I offer peace to that person instead and do the uncomfortable work of reconciling. I remember that harmony isn't silence; it's different sounds coming together to create beautiful music. It's a genuine expression of oneself, while at the same time moving towards another's expression of herself.

Instead of shooting for world peace or trying to write an entire score of four-part harmony, we can put in motion a small ripple of peace today. Is there someone we can greet with a smile instead of moving to the other side of the street? Is there a phone call we've been putting off that we can enter into in a spirit of prayer? Is there a chance to light a small corner that is dark because it does not know the Light?

We are children of God, given the grace to call him Father and everything that comes with that adoption. He gathers us close, breathes the spirit of peace upon us, and sends us out to do his will in a weary world in need of reconciliation.

Elizabeth Foss

WEDNESDAY OF THE SECOND WEEK OF LENT

OPEN YOUR BIBLE Matthew 5:10-12

"Blessed are those who are persecuted for righteousness' sake, for theirs is the kingdom of heaven.

"Blessed are you when people revile you and persecute you and utter all kinds of evil against you falsely on my account. Rejoice and be glad, for your reward is great in heaven, for in the same way they persecuted the prophets who were before you."

NOTES

FOR FURTHER READING MATTHEW 5:43-45

THEIRS IS THE KINGDOM OF HEAVEN

A PROMISE OF LOVE ▶ Blessed are those who are persecuted for righteousness' sake, for theirs is the kingdom of heaven. ◀ THE BEATITUDE

◀ THE ETERNAL VALUE

What does it mean to be persecuted for righteousness' sake?	What kind of transformation of the inner person is being asked of you by this beatitude?	Define the characteristics of **SELF-CONTROL**

The beatitudes present a way of life that promises salvation and peace in the midst of the trials and tribulations on earth. How can you live this beatitude here and now?

Refer to the chart on pages 32 and 33 for more info on how to interpret the beatitudes.

BLESSED ARE THOSE WHO ARE PERSECUTED FOR RIGHTEOUSNESS' SAKE

a promise of love

wednesday of the second week of lent

It's all too good to believe. Heaven. Eternal reward. The wedding feast of the Lamb. Many mansions and streets paved with gold. All of it is just too good.

And the conditions for our souls—the way we need to live our lives in order to be open to this blessing? Too hard. Too out of reach. Can't be done in our power.

Is that why we are a post-Christian society? Is that why the people who are accepting—embracing even—of new age practices, abortion on demand, sex without commitment (and sometimes without affection) are scornful of Christianity? They believe the lies and they take aim at the truth behind the shields of their cultural superiority, using spears barbed with their sarcasm. Do they have no imagination for the promises of Christ, no fortitude for the moral imperatives of the beatitudes, that they accept nothing that can't be proven and rely entirely on the self-sufficiency of their intellectualism?

We are not martyrs being fed to the lions, but we are persecuted daily as our way of life is maligned by the majority and derided by those who believe themselves to be academically enlightened.

The gospel is for the broken, not the arrogant souls who think they have it all figured out. The good news is that Christ came for the lame and the weak and the poor and the suffering. We cannot receive him unless we acknowledge that we need him for our every breath. We cannot enter into Good Friday unless we are willing to have our bones broken as we hang upon a cross. We won't be healed until we admit that we are mortally ill. And we cannot rise on a glorious Easter morning unless we have our thirst met by rags soaked in vinegar. What a crazy thing it is to give the assent of our will to be a follower of Jesus!

When we give our *fiat* to a life with and for Christ, we give our assent to persecution for his name's sake—whatever form that might take. This makes me a little afraid, to be honest. Some days, it makes me more than a little afraid. Perhaps it does you too? Do you worry and wonder what you will suffer in order to answer the call of your vocation? Do you ever look at the neighbor who chose an easy path dictated by an entirely secular perspective on success—the one who eats, drinks, and is merry without so much as a nod to inevitable death—and wonder if maybe you are just a misguided glutton for punishment?

But what if it's all true? What if the gospel is really, truly true? What if there is a God who created us for eternity and there is a glorious heaven and there is the punishment of hell?

If it's all true, then the way that we live right now matters enormously. When we die, we will be judged on how we loved. God will look at us with love and all eternity will hinge on whether we can raise our eyes to return his gaze.

Our Lord is a patient teacher. He wants nothing more than for us to learn to love, and he will keep teaching us for as long as we have breath. So often, we are the worst impediments to the lessons he has for us. Puffed up by our perceived knowledge, paralyzed by our own self-importance, and stymied by a lack of empathy, we fail to love. He meets us there. He grants us the grace to move beyond ourselves to the transcendence of his Holy Spirit and there, if we let him, he teaches us to love. There, if we let him reveal it to us, we catch a glimpse of the kingdom of heaven here on this broken earth.

Elizabeth Foss

THURSDAY OF THE SECOND WEEK OF LENT

OPEN YOUR BIBLE Matthew 5:21-26

"You have heard that it was said to those of ancient times, 'You shall not murder'; and 'whoever murders shall be liable to judgment.' But I say to you that if you are angry with a brother or sister, you will be liable to judgment; and if you insult a brother or sister, you will be liable to the council; and if you say, 'You fool,' you will be liable to the hell of fire. So when you are offering your gift at the altar, if you remember that your brother or sister has something against you, leave your gift there before the altar and go; first be reconciled to your brother or sister, and then come and offer your gift. Come to terms quickly with your accuser while you are on the way to court with him, or your accuser may hand you over to the judge, and the judge to the guard, and you will be thrown into prison. Truly I tell you, you will never get out until you have paid the last penny."

NOTES

FOR FURTHER READING MATTHEW 5:45-48

LECTIO DIVINA

hosanna

What is Jesus saying or doing in this passage?

What does this passage reveal to me about God's mercy?

In what area of my life do I need to hear this message of mercy?

thursday of the second week of lent

Do you remember the old saying, "Sticks and stones may break my bones but words will never hurt me"? It's the first thing that came to mind when reading today's Scripture passages. How many times have I spouted it throughout my life as a defense when I have been belittled or wounded by something someone has said about me?

Too many to count.

The words we speak and the actions we take have incredible power. They either give life or take it away. When spoken or acted on in anger or without consideration of the tenderness of the human heart, they can destroy. In Matthew's Gospel, Jesus has just completed the Sermon on the Mount, spelling out for the people how to live a good Christian life. In the passages shared here, he digs a little deeper, admonishing the sinner to be careful about what she harbors in her heart and how she thinks and speaks about her neighbor. He instructs that we are to make things right with our neighbor if we have harmed them with our words or actions. Without doing so, we cannot repair the breach our sin has caused in our relationship with God himself.

How many times have I thought ill of my neighbor or even my friend? How many times has my tongue betrayed my heart filled with jealousy and spite?

Too many to count.

Every time I read this passage my stomach rolls. It's as if Jesus is speaking directly to me. I am a passionate woman, equally prone to outbursts of anger as of joy. There is not much about me that you will find in between. I am also prone to holding a grudge. It's real, and it's not attractive.

Recently a friend of mine made a decision that impacted me quite negatively, leaving me feeling angry and taken advantage of. I sat with those feelings for almost two weeks, allowing them to fester and create more discord by the day. My father used to say that anger and unforgiveness only rot the vessel in which they are contained. I realized my vessel was rotting and that I needed to clean it all out.

When I brought my hurt and anger to the Lord in prayer, I discovered a severe lack of humility on my part. Jesus taught that in order to receive forgiveness for what we have done, we must offer forgiveness for what has been done to us. I knew I had to forgive her for what she had done. Forgiveness is a decision of the will, not an emotion. The hurt would still be present, but if forgiveness was given, then I could let go of the anger and work my way through those jumbled feelings and residual pain. I could learn to trust her again.

I gathered the courage to speak with her, not knowing how she would react. I had to trust that no matter what happened, God would be present and he would honor my efforts to follow his lead. It was awkward at first, but the more I opened up, the more she shared. In the end, mercy was shown, forgiveness given and received freely, and grace abounded. Our relationship was restored and I am ever grateful for it. We began again that day, much like we do every time we go to confession or forgive ourselves.

Is there someone in your life you need to forgive? Don't allow that anger and pain to continue to fester, rotting all that is good within you. Be courageous, looking to the cross for the answer—"Father, forgive them, for they know not what they do." Allow his mercy to reign in your heart, for he offered his life for it.

Mary Lenaburg

FRIDAY OF THE SECOND WEEK OF LENT

OPEN YOUR BIBLE Matthew 6:1-4

"Beware of practicing your piety before others in order to be seen by them; for then you have no reward from your Father in heaven.

"So whenever you give alms, do not sound a trumpet before you, as the hypocrites do in the synagogues and in the streets, so that they may be praised by others. Truly I tell you, they have received their reward. But when you give alms, do not let your left hand know what your right hand is doing, so that your alms may be done in secret; and your Father who sees in secret will reward you."

NOTES

FOR FURTHER READING MATTHEW 6:16-18

LECTIO DIVINA

hosanna

What is Jesus saying or doing in this passage?

What does this passage reveal to me about God's mercy?

In what area of my life do I need to hear this message of mercy?

friday of the second week of lent

It was December in Arizona, and it was cold. Colder than cold. We had walked nine miles, descended an altitude of 4,500 feet, and the temperature hardly reached the double digits. Bundled in a fleece-lined trench coat, I could just barely stave off the chill as my travel companions and I sat underneath the clearest night sky you could imagine. I'll go out on a limb and say there is no better place to grasp the magnitude of the universe than at the base of the Grand Canyon.

I had spent the previous four months working and living in a homeless shelter. We served a community of pregnant woman who were often recovering from addiction. I had no idea what to expect when I walked in the front door on that first August evening, but I certainly did not anticipate the overwhelming sense of belonging I found amidst my new family.

Rarely do we notice when things are easy. We wake up and go to sleep in a familiar bed, often near people we love and who care for us. We spend our days going about the mundane, forgetting that what is a small burden to us could be a remarkable blessing to others.

My time at the homeless shelter quickly snapped life into perspective. That evening in the base of the Grand Canyon, when I was cold and hungry and sore, was an immense privilege. I had chosen to walk a challenging road with fully-functioning legs, and the next day, I walked out of that somewhat less-than-perfect situation and back into the comfort of my home, bed, and lifestyle. If only we could all be so lucky.

But it's all temporary. Remember you are dust, and to dust you shall return. Whatever do we do with that?

As we travel deeper into the Lenten season, we are reminded of our call to practice piety. We are reminded of the call to serve others. We are reminded of the call to give alms with humility and secrecy. It is not about denying our privilege but using it to aid others in a way that is not belittling or patronizing. It is about recognizing that at any moment, life can change.

So how do we live in a way that prepares us for that potential shift, for that phone call that changes it all, or for that unexpected move or that inevitable breakup?

We give alms. We sound no trumpets. We do not seek what is earthly, but what is everlasting.

The night's sleep in my cabin seemed too short. I was awakened by my friend pounding on my door, an hour earlier than we had agreed upon. He was up with the sun and eager to start the trek back. It had never been the descent into the Grand Canyon that posed the challenge. With every bend of the trail, we had encountered another hiker whose short breath and exasperated greeting reminded us of our impending fate. What goes up has to come down, right? In regards to the Grand Canyon, the opposite is true.

As members of a faith familiar with pain, we are encouraged to offer up our suffering. We are often reminded to offer it up on those seemingly extra-long days of fasting during Lent. It does little good to fast if we spend the day complaining of our hunger. Rather, we use it as a time to repent and seek God's mercy.

On my journey up the South Rim, I realized pretty quickly that, to make it back up, I would be offering a lot up: the cramping of my calves, the tightness in my lungs, the never-ending path ahead. It's not easy to find joy in suffering. But oh, how much easier it makes the journey.

Carly Buckholz

SELAH

PAUSE
PRAYER
PRAISE
REST

I will recount the gracious deeds of the LORD, the praiseworthy acts of the LORD, because of all that the LORD has done for us, / and the great favor to the house of Israel / that he has shown them according to his mercy, according to the abundance of his steadfast love.

Isaiah 63:7

Check in.

TODAY'S DATE	PLACE OF PEACE:
_____	_____	_____	_____

I'M FEELING

- ○ happy
- ○ excited
- ○ joyful

- ○ anxious
- ○ upset
- ○ tired

- ○ annoyed
- ○ angry
- ○ sad

- ○ grateful
- ○ confused
- ○ calm

- ○ _____
- ○ _____
- ○ _____

Outside my window:

Small successes:

Giving thanks for:

Working on my heart:

Listening to:

In my prayers:

Hope for next week:

"Blessed are the pure in heart,
for they will see God."

MATTHEW 5:8

scripture memory

MATTHEW 5:7-8

"Blessed are the merciful,
for they will receive mercy.

"Blessed are the pure in heart,
for they will see God."

I will practice Scripture memory by:
- ◯ Praying
- ◯ Writing
- ◯ Speaking
- ◯ Reading
- ◯ Other: _____

OPEN YOUR BIBLE

Matthew 6:5-10

"And whenever you pray, do not be like the hypocrites; for they love to stand and pray in the synagogues and at the street corners, so that they may be seen by others. Truly I tell you, they have received their reward. But whenever you pray, go into your room and shut the door and pray to your Father who is in secret; and your Father who sees in secret will reward you.

"When you are praying, do not heap up empty phrases as the Gentiles do; for they think that they will be heard because of their many words. Do not be like them, for your Father knows what you need before you ask him.

"Pray then in this way:

Our Father in heaven,
hallowed be your name.
Your kingdom come.
Your will be done,
on earth as it is in heaven."

NOTES

FOR FURTHER READING MATTHEW 6:19-21

LECTIO DIVINA

hosanna

What is Jesus saying or doing in this passage?

What does this passage reveal to me about God's mercy?

In what area of my life do I need to hear this message of mercy?

I have decided that nine children is enough people to make a respectable "scientific" sample size. All nine of my children, when learning the Lord's Prayer, have said, "hallowed be my name. My kingdom come, my will be done." I don't know if it's just that they have no context for the word "thy" in their young lives or if they've been given a childlike understanding of one of humankind's greatest failings. I just know it's a universal truth—that instead of laying down our cognizant, conscious wills to live in the will of God, we hallow our own names instead. And that's just an uphill climb with failure at the top.

My hope for those children is that they will grow into a unique understanding of their calling in life. Jesus invites each of them— and each of us—into a partnership with him to further the kingdom of heaven here on earth. That's a pretty awesome call, if only we can get out of our own way and not persist in hallowing our names instead of his.

Here on earth, I am given foretastes of heaven: the feel of a newborn, soft and warm in my arms after the hard work of labor; the smell of basil and tomato in my grandmother's well-worn kitchen; and the flicker of recognition in my father's eyes in the brief moment before dementia again stakes its claim. We find our truest moments of nearness to the glory of heaven when we are gathered in a community of believers to pray and sing and worship and break bread together. Cooperating with God in the co-creation of life, honoring the sick and the aged as image-bearers of the Lord, and living as the apostles did, we see up close the good that God intends for us.

In stark contrast are the moments when I substitute my will for God's. The sense of alienation I feel when I am selfish is the pain of separation from the kingdom. I live in the tension of wanting to know and do the Lord's will but not always knowing what that will is or not always succeeding in surrendering to it. In those moments of fervent prayer, I can offer him myself, soul made tender in the Sacrament of Confession, and ask him to pour into me the grace of knowing him. He will make his will clear if I ask and if I am patient in the waiting for his answer.

It is always difficult to put down the pen and let God be the rightful author of my story. I think I know exactly how each plot twist and each turn of phrase should go. But if I do it—if I let God be God and I just the instrument in his hands—he astounds me every time with his mercy, his grace, and his abundance. God will not be outdone by my imagination. His will for my life is infinitely more beautiful than any story I can conjure.

As I write, I think of a dear friend whose life is in shambles right now. Horror and tragedy have settled on her family and she is understandably distraught. I look at the circumstances from my objective distance and I reread the paragraph above this one. She didn't override God's will. Instead, someone in her life abused free will and brought harm to her and to people she loves. The ripples of this evil spread wide. The pain inflicted by someone else will be felt by generations.

How does she hold faith in such circumstances? Where is God when it hurts? He is right there with her in the pain. Right there. He knows what it is to be abused, to be violated, and to be beaten to the point of death. He knows what it is to have evil snuff out life on earth.

And he rose.

He rose for her, so that she can hope in the hurt and have joy in the future.

If you offer your life to the Lord and want to live for him, he will prevail.

Every time.

Lord, we believe. Help our unbelief.

Elizabeth Foss

TUESDAY OF THE THIRD WEEK OF LENT

OPEN YOUR BIBLE Matthew 6:11-14

"Give us this day our daily bread.

And forgive us our debts,

as we also have forgiven our debtors.

And do not bring us to the time of trial,

but rescue us from the evil one.

For if you forgive others their trespasses,

your heavenly Father will also forgive you."

NOTES

FOR FURTHER READING MATTHEW 6:22-24

LECTIO DIVINA

hosanna

What is Jesus saying or doing in this passage?

What does this passage reveal to me about God's mercy?

In what area of my life do I need to hear this message of mercy?

tuesday of the third week of lent

My grandmother once told me that with every baby comes a loaf of bread. What she meant to encourage in me is the trust that if we are open to God's plans for our lives, he will provide what we need when we need it. It is a wisdom that has borne itself out in the three decades that I've been married.

When God crafted me into a human being, he blessed me with an enhanced sense of perception. I notice detail in nearly everything: spoken words, the nuance of a text message (seems like an oxymoron, right?), and the scene in a public square or at Costco on a busy Sunday. I'm there for it, present and perceptive. He also blessed me with an imagination—with the ability to think ahead of the current moment and imagine all sorts of scenarios, many of them ridiculously problematic. Both the blessings serve me well as a writer. People with perception and imagination who are also able to turn a phrase have the unique joy of putting into words the stuff of experiences we all hold in common.

But this combination of abilities can also lead me far astray of God's intended path of blessing. I'm able to project all kinds of worry into all kinds of situations. If I'm not careful, I can rush headlong into a storm of what-ifs that leave me breathless and terrified. God will provide for this day. I need to stay in the moment and turn my attention to how I can cooperate with his will in the here and now.

Further, I need to turn my attention away from myself and towards others. Jesus tells us to ask the Father for our daily bread. He will provide for me, and if I cooperate with him and look for the opportunities, he will also provide ways for me nourish others, both physically and spiritually.

Well-nourished, I beg the Lord to protect me from temptation. Evil is real. It lurks, clever and conniving, determined to lure me into its snares. And evil lurks around all the people I love. If they can be drawn into its nefarious web, I will suffer also. And the devil is well aware that despair is a useful tool to lure a mother into the desert of temptation. Resist evil. Be firm and persistent in prayer, and resist the desert of temptation. You do not have to engage in spiritual warfare alone. Look up. Look out. Join forces with other Christians. Hold each other accountable and be an encouragement to one another.

It is in this outward focus that I am also able to live out the words of the final phrases of the prayer. Jesus says that if I forgive those who have offended me, the Father will forgive me. Honestly, there's not a lot of nuance here. He's very direct. Look up. Look out. Forgive. And in forgiving, release the grip of sin on my own life.

The Father waits, wanting to hear my confession. He waits, wanting to forgive me. We forgive and we are forgiven. But there is one more dimension to forgiveness. Jesus wants us to forgive ourselves. We set standards for ourselves that are not at all what God intended. We miss the fact that he knew we would fail, and he entered into that relationship of forgiveness with us. When we fail to forgive ourselves, we usurp God's role and we deal with his people (ourselves) without mercy. This beautiful prayer that Jesus prays to his Father teaches us to let God be God, and to surrender ourselves to his tender mercy and provision.

Elizabeth Foss

WEDNESDAY OF THE THIRD WEEK OF LENT

OPEN YOUR BIBLE Matthew 7:1-5

"Do not judge, so that you may not be judged. For with the judgment you make you will be judged, and the measure you give will be the measure you get. Why do you see the speck in your neighbor's eye, but do not notice the log in your own eye? Or how can you say to your neighbor, 'Let me take the speck out of your eye,' while the log is in your own eye? You hypocrite, first take the log out of your own eye, and then you will see clearly to take the speck out of your neighbor's eye."

NOTES

FOR FURTHER READING MATTHEW 7:24-29

LECTIO DIVINA

hosanna

What is Jesus saying or doing in this passage?

What does this passage reveal to me about God's mercy?

In what area of my life do I need to hear this message of mercy?

wednesday of the third week of lent

Last year when I made the transition from living in the rainforests of Costa Rica to the not-so-rainy or foresty neighborhoods of Indiana, my body went into a bit of shock and did not take all that well to the adjustment. One of the first signs was a massive and long-lived eye infection that left me with upper eyelids bulging with styes numbering in the twenties below them. Here is the infuriating thing about painful eyes: your brain constantly convinces you that if you just close them everything will be better. Then you close them. And it feels better. For about two milliseconds. And then it just feels a different version of the miserable it feels when they are open.

This, I think, might be a bit like what happens when sin has wedged itself in our spiritual eyes. We long to be able to look away—to close our eyes and make it go away—to do anything but deal with the actual culprit that has made us miserable and uncomfortable. So, with our vision blurred and our eyes half-opened, we are tempted to point our fingers at someone else, thinking that if we could just shut our eyelids on our own spiritual discomfort, we could feel better.

And we do. For just a moment. There is that one instant of self-satisfaction when we justify our own mess by pointing out someone else's. But the reality is that looking away, closing our eyes, pointing our finger in the other direction—none of it works. None of it will cure us because the irritant remains, and as long as there is still the smallest speck of sin wedged into our spiritual eyes, we will feel the burn—the instinctive desire to get rid of it and ease our discomfort.

Christ's admonition here—"Do not judge, so that you may not be judged" (Matthew 7:1)—is less an attempt to scare us into doing what he wants us to do and more of a question, I think. I think to myself that he is asking me very important questions. What do you think you are gaining by pointing out someone else's sin? Are you any closer to heaven for it? Any more deeply immersed in my mercy and my grace?

What if, instead of diverting and deflecting, we opened our spiritual eyes, found the source of irritation, and got rid of it—removed it? What if we stopped trying to use that wounded and weepy eye to examine everyone else and instead acknowledged that it needs healing?

Sometimes I feel like the "do not judge" conversation is an unending loop in Christian circles. People feel judged for being told not to judge and start judging the people who told them not to judge. This, I think, may be what Christ is pointing at in the first few verses here. It is he who engages in the judgment spiral with us, but we who spin circles around one another. The harsher we become, the worse the criticism that gets hurled back at us becomes. You only need about two minutes and a Facebook account to see this played out a million times over every day.

The problem is this: no one is made any better for it. Only in self-examination can we be brought to freedom. An honest look at our own spiritual blindness and its cause is the only path to relief. We can't close our eyes. We can't look away. We can't squint and point fingers. We've got to be still, open our eyes, and take a long look at ourselves. The good news? The irritating culprit of sin is usually so large and so obvious that once we do look, the remedy becomes clear.

Colleen Connell

THURSDAY OF THE THIRD WEEK OF LENT

OPEN YOUR BIBLE Matthew 8:5-13

When he entered Capernaum, a centurion came to him, appealing to him and saying, "Lord, my servant is lying at home paralyzed, in terrible distress." And he said to him, "I will come and cure him." The centurion answered, "Lord, I am not worthy to have you come under my roof; but only speak the word, and my servant will be healed. For I also am a man under authority, with soldiers under me; and I say to one, 'Go,' and he goes, and to another, 'Come,' and he comes, and to my slave, 'Do this,' and the slave does it." When Jesus heard him, he was amazed and said to those who followed him, "Truly I tell you, in no one in Israel have I found such faith. I tell you, many will come from east and west and will eat with Abraham and Isaac and Jacob in the kingdom of heaven, while the heirs of the kingdom will be thrown into the outer darkness, where there will be weeping and gnashing of teeth." And to the centurion Jesus said, "Go; let it be done for you according to your faith." And the servant was healed in that hour.

NOTES

FOR FURTHER READING MATTHEW 8:23-27

LECTIO DIVINA

hosanna

What is Jesus saying or doing in this passage?

What does this passage reveal to me about God's mercy?

In what area of my life do I need to hear this message of mercy?

thursday of the third week of lent

A dear friend of mine recently got married, and as she walked down the aisle, glowing with happiness, I was overcome with emotion, remembering how sorrowful and sick she'd been just a few years earlier. It was not only her healing that brought me to tears, but also the memory of some of the most raw and heartfelt words I've ever prayed, which I prayed for her.

My husband and I were in Lourdes, France when we received her sobering email, sharing that the chemotherapy wasn't working as expected. Even though we'd just left the grotto an hour earlier, we wordlessly got up and began the short walk back. It was nearly empty when we arrived, so I walked right in and put my hand on the wall, touching the water that trickled down from the miraculous spring. A boldness rose up within me and, through loud sobs, I begged and pleaded with God to spare my friend's life. From the details she'd shared, I knew that her prognosis was not good. But in my desperation I held nothing back, trusting that God in his mercy and power was fully capable of healing her if it was his will.

Recalling those prayers has made me realize how infrequently I pray for myself with the same wild abandon and complete trust. I've struggled with one health issue after another over the past few years, and while I ask God to help me make it through, I don't ask for complete healing though it's what I truly long for. My prayers are often timid and not fully reflective of all that's in my heart.

I'd like to think that this is because of humility and faith—that because I want what God wants and trust that he knows best, I simply pray that his will be done. But in truth I don't pray for complete healing because I don't fully trust that I'm worthy of it. I see my sins and shortcomings as bigger than his mercy, which is just another form of pride. Plus, I worry that if I'm not healed, I won't be able to handle the disappointment.

When the centurion longs for his servant to be healed, he too acknowledges his unworthiness. But he doesn't see it as a stumbling block to God's mercy because he understands that we're all unworthy, and that it's God's grace that allows anyone at all to receive his mercy. He also trusts that God's mercy and love is bigger than our sinfulness—for who is he to question the goodness of the Son of God? And so in the same breath he acknowledges his complete faith in a God who is not only merciful but also all-powerful and able to heal any of his children completely.

The centurion's humble and pure faith is a powerful example of how we too should come to God in prayer. Each time we echo his words at Mass, it's an opportunity to affirm our trust in God. In particular, the words "my soul shall be healed" remind us that sometimes physical healing is not God's will. Sometimes, he sanctifies us through suffering or asks us to partake in the salvation of others by offering up our suffering for them. His ways are not ours, and we do not always understand them. But he is always good, and he will never abandon us in our suffering.

Jesus' amazement at the centurion's faith suggests that the centurion understood this too. And yet, though he knew that the answer might be no, he still came to Jesus with his deepest longing. He held nothing back. May we follow his example and boldly share our hearts freely with God, and in humility trust in his unending love and mercy.

Allison McGinley

FRIDAY OF THE THIRD WEEK OF LENT

OPEN YOUR BIBLE Matthew 9:14-17

Then the disciples of John came to him, saying, "Why do we and the Pharisees fast often, but your disciples do not fast?" And Jesus said to them, "The wedding guests cannot mourn as long as the bridegroom is with them, can they? The days will come when the bridegroom is taken away from them, and then they will fast. No one sews a piece of unshrunk cloth on an old cloak, for the patch pulls away from the cloak, and a worse tear is made. Neither is new wine put into old wineskins; otherwise, the skins burst, and the wine is spilled, and the skins are destroyed; but new wine is put into fresh wineskins, and so both are preserved."

NOTES

FOR FURTHER READING ▶ MATTHEW 9:9-13

LECTIO DIVINA

hosanna

What is Jesus saying or doing in this passage?

What does this passage reveal to me about God's mercy?

In what area of my life do I need to hear this message of mercy?

friday of the third week of lent

I struggle with self-care. My mantra is "you get out what you put in." If you want to be loved, love. If you want to see a project through, work hard. If you want people to invest in you, invest in them. If you put good things into the world, they will come back. I find much truth in this philosophy.

Thank God it isn't God's.

It's early 2019 and over the past month my Christmas gifts would have made a great movie montage. A coworker gave me tea with a reminder to relax. Friends gave me books on meditation. My best friend gave me a contraption that looked like a supersized plastic horseshoe—it was a neck massager. The "stress relief" lotion that came with it was a not-so-subtle hint. Her boyfriend told me that my word for 2019 needed to be "no." My sister told me that my resolution needed to be to "sleep like an actual adult." I've noticed it too—my skin is a mess. I'm snapping when someone asks me the smallest favor. I'm not usually a big cryer, but these days I'm seconds from tears.

By not taking care of myself I'm causing my tribe to worry. I find this a little funny because I thought I was doing an okay job of hiding my emptiness. No, kid. Your Christmas gifts had a theme. The disciples of John ask Jesus why his followers aren't fasting like they do, and I don't even have that altruistic excuse. I'm just fasting because I'm overextended.

The trick with my philosophy of "getting out what you put in," of course, is that "you can't pour from an empty cup." I hate that phrase. I hate that it's true. Jesus says it better: "No one sews a piece of unshrunk cloth on an old cloak, for the patch pulls away from the cloak, and a worse tear is made" (Matthew 9:16). It's less quotable but I like it because it implies that you can't make repairs when you aren't healthy yourself—you might actually do more harm than good. That scares me more—by trying to help when you're not ready, you might be doing damage.

Right now I think God's telling me two things. First, that sometimes in saying "yes"—even though "yes" is courageous and vulnerable—I am not ready, and I will fail, and I need to admit that. Part of a prayer on the wall in Mother Teresa's home for children in Calcutta reads: "Give the best you have, and it will never be enough. Give your best anyway." This humility is an exceptionally difficult pill for me to swallow. Second, God is reminding me that he gave me the feeling to say "yes" in the first place for a reason. Life takes a village. He's telling me to ask for help. My self-care isn't bath bombs and thirty minutes to scroll through Instagram. It's listening to my friends and family. It's getting sleep. It's noticing how good my body feels after I take a brisk walk. It's reminding myself that failure is part of life and extending grace to myself when I falter.

Depleting your resources completely, all the time, will not allow you to serve God's kingdom to your full potential. It is not selfish to sleep nor, if you've been gifted with this wisdom, is it egotistical to say "no." It is not weakness to ask for help. Women need to hear these messages over and over again.

Take care of yourself. When the new wine is ready to be poured, you don't want to burst with the filling. You want to be fresh and ready to preserve that goodness.

Katy Greiner

SELAH

PAUSE
PRAYER
PRAISE
REST

Thus says the LORD who made the earth, the LORD who formed it to establish it—the LORD is his name: Call to me and I will answer you, and will tell you great and hidden things that you have not known.

Jeremiah 33:2-3

Check in.

TODAY'S DATE	PLACE OF PEACE:
___|___|___	_____

I'M FEELING

- ○ happy
- ○ excited
- ○ joyful

- ○ anxious
- ○ upset
- ○ tired

- ○ annoyed
- ○ angry
- ○ sad

- ○ grateful
- ○ confused
- ○ calm

- ○ _____
- ○ _____
- ○ _____

Outside my window:

_____

Small successes:

Working on my heart:

_____

Listening to:

_____

In my prayers:

Giving thanks for:

Hope for next week:

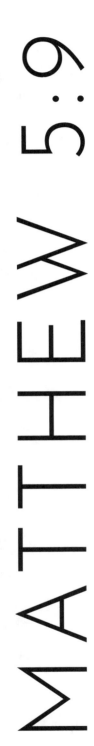

MATTHEW 5:9

"Blessed are the peacemakers,
for they will be called children of God."

scripture memory

MATTHEW 5:9-10

"Blessed are the peacemakers,
for they will be called children of God.

Blessed are those who are persecuted for righteousness' sake,
for theirs is the kingdom of heaven."

I will practice Scripture memory by:
- ○ Praying
- ○ Writing
- ○ Speaking
- ○ Reading
- ○ Other: _____

MONDAY OF THE FOURTH WEEK OF LENT

OPEN YOUR BIBLE Matthew 10:16-33

"See, I am sending you out like sheep into the midst of wolves; so be wise as serpents and innocent as doves. Beware of them, for they will hand you over to councils and flog you in their synagogues; and you will be dragged before governors and kings because of me, as a testimony to them and the Gentiles. When they hand you over, do not worry about how you are to speak or what you are to say; for what you are to say will be given to you at that time; for it is not you who speak, but the Spirit of your Father speaking through you. Brother will betray brother to death, and a father his child, and children will rise against parents and have them put to death; and you will be hated by all because of my name. But the one who endures to the end will be saved. When they persecute you in one town, flee to the next; for truly I tell you, you will not have gone through all the towns of Israel before the Son of Man comes.

"A disciple is not above the teacher, nor a slave above the master; it is enough for the disciple to be like the teacher, and the slave like the master. If they have called the master of the house Beelzebul, how much more will they malign those of his household!

"So have no fear of them; for nothing is covered up that will not be uncovered, and nothing secret that will not become known. What I say to you in the dark, tell in the light; and what you hear whispered, proclaim from the housetops. Do not fear those who kill the body but cannot kill the soul; rather fear him who can destroy both soul and body in hell. Are not two sparrows sold for a penny? Yet not one of them will fall to the ground apart from your Father. And even the hairs of your head are all counted. So do not be afraid; you are of more value than many sparrows.

"Everyone therefore who acknowledges me before others, I also will acknowledge before my Father in heaven; but whoever denies me before others, I also will deny before my Father in heaven."

FOR FURTHER READING MATTHEW 10:5-15

LECTIO DIVINA

hosanna

What is Jesus saying or doing in the passage?

What does this passage reveal to me about God's mercy?

In what area of my life do I need to hear this message of mercy?

monday of the fourth week of lent

"I am sending you out like sheep into the midst of wolves" (Matthew 10:16). That's how today's reading starts. It's not very comforting, is it? Have you ever seen what a pack of hungry wolves can do to a sheep? Those poor sheep are torn apart and completely consumed.

If social media and the last presidential election have taught me anything, it's how bloodthirsty the people I love can really be. I refused to publicly state how I'd voted, and was savaged by lifelong friends and family members. People stopped talking to me for the things they assumed I believed, and all the things I wouldn't say. I loved many of them dearly, how could they turn on me like this?

That election taught me not to discuss my political views in public unless I was willing to take the punishment. For some time after that, I was wary of saying anything publicly which might be seen as controversial. All that just over politics. When the topic turns to God, faith, and religion, people lose their minds. Truth isn't always socially acceptable, and it can be harrowing to stand up alone against the world.

But we're not alone, are we? God, in his mercy, doesn't send us out without sending the Holy Spirit along with us. He promises: "Do not worry about how you are to speak or what you are to say; for what you are to say will be given to you at that time; for it is not you who speak, but the Spirit of your Father speaking through you" (Matthew 10:19-20). God doesn't put us out there to be eaten alive when he sends us out as his representatives to a tired and sinful world. Even our weaknesses and imperfections aren't a problem. We don't have to know what to say or how to say it before we go. We just have to go.

Recently, a work client of mine was telling me of her weekend plans. She's an atheist, and her beliefs are as opposite to Church social teaching as it's possible to get, but she's also someone I can't afford to offend. "I'm taking my kids to the Pride parade this weekend," she told me. "What are you doing?"

I paused for a moment, wondering how much of my Catholic "weirdness" to out in this particular moment. I paused long enough for the Holy Spirit to nudge me to just tell her everything. "I'm taking my kids on a pilgrimage to see the remains of St. Maria Goretti." And then I waited.

She wasn't put off. She was fascinated. Every question she asked was one that I had an answer to, many of them answers I didn't know that I knew.

I wish I could say that she converted on the spot or that I'd led her to rethink her militant atheism. She hasn't yet but who knows what will happen in the future. That conversation, and those that followed, have led her to become much less hostile to Christianity as a whole, and to Catholicism in particular.

Speaking and living our faith out loud is easy when we're with like-minded people. It's much harder when we know the social price that we will pay for being openly Catholic in a secular world. We have been culturally conditioned to fear the societal "sin" of offending others and to do anything possible to avoid it.

It can be tempting to be silent and hope to slip through life unnoticed and unharmed, but Jesus warns us about the cowardice of doing so: "Everyone therefore who acknowledges me before others, I also will acknowledge before my Father in heaven; but whoever denies me before others, I also will deny before my Father in heaven" (Matthew 10:32–33). We have to allow God to be bigger than our fears. Eternity depends on it.

Rebecca Frech

TUESDAY OF THE FOURTH WEEK OF LENT

OPEN YOUR BIBLE Matthew 11:25-30

At that time Jesus said, "I thank you, Father, Lord of heaven and earth, because you have hidden these things from the wise and the intelligent and have revealed them to infants; yes, Father, for such was your gracious will. All things have been handed over to me by my Father; and no one knows the Son except the Father, and no one knows the Father except the Son and anyone to whom the Son chooses to reveal him.

"Come to me, all you that are weary and are carrying heavy burdens, and I will give you rest. Take my yoke upon you, and learn from me; for I am gentle and humble in heart, and you will find rest for your souls. For my yoke is easy, and my burden is light."

NOTES

FOR FURTHER READING MATTHEW 11:7-19

LECTIO DIVINA

hosanna

What is Jesus saying or doing in this passage?

What does this passage reveal to me about God's mercy?

In what area of my life do I need to hear this message of mercy?

tuesday of the fourth week of lent

Mid-afternoon, it was time to take the eldest to ballet lessons. The routine with my other daughter was a little date at a coffee shop for treats in that hour space of time between drop-off and pick-up for ballet. But I was reconsidering our plans.

I'd been rushing from one task to another all day, trying so hard to earn those check marks next to each of the items on the to-do list, but the oversight of rambunctious children had made this nearly impossible. She certainly hadn't earned her treat; her behavior more resembled the monkeys in the zoo than a well-mannered child. I was considering having her hearing checked due to her lack of attention to nearly every word spoken to her. Perhaps we would simply use the time for errands and she could stay strapped into her seat for deserved containment purposes.

However, when I took a quiet moment for consideration between the cries for "one more chance!" that still, small voice in the recesses of my heart whispered to me that this was not the right choice. We both needed a break. We both needed to stop a moment and just rest in each other's presence.

We parked near one of our favorite paths and took a walk in the brisk air and warm sunshine to shake off the inner cobwebs. She tugged my hand, leading me to the literal webs fantastically spun along the bars of the bridge. We paused to admire a swarm of gulls making loops over and over, way above our heads. She shared all the things on her heart as we strolled along. In the end, I allowed her the treat at the café after all, as those moments of resting in each other's presence had seemed to wash away the tension between us.

The Lord beckons us to rest. In fact, for our good, he commands it. The siren call of the busy cries out from the opposite direction—one more chore, one more check mark on the to-do list!

Stopping to rest in him, we can find peace. Remaining in the constant hustle, we find worry and anxiety.

There, in his presence, we find our burdens relieved. In the swirl of the hustle, the burdens pile on and on.

Will you let go and let him? The Lord is calling out to you, "Come to me, all you that are weary and are carrying heavy burdens, and I will give you rest" (Matthew 11:28). Don't grip so tightly all that needs to be done. Have faith and release into his hands, with a humble heart, all that burdens you.

Connection calls us to be present; being present requires that we rest from the hustle. I could not be truly present and connect with my daughter that day until I had intentionally laid it all down and turned my heart toward her. It was a moment of grace as her heart, reciprocally, turned toward mine. She begged for mercy and I readily gave it. But it required a full stop. I wanted to chase down all my work until it was no more, but ironically, it was in the laying down that I found the ability to carry it to completion later on.

All the more so, the Lord desires the same of our hearts. He is readily waiting and constantly available to connect, to embrace, to relieve, to love, and to dole out mercy beyond what we could ever imagine. It simply requires rest.

Laurel Muff

WEDNESDAY OF THE FOURTH WEEK OF LENT

OPEN YOUR BIBLE Matthew 12:22-32

Then they brought to him a demoniac who was blind and mute; and he cured him, so that the one who had been mute could speak and see. All the crowds were amazed and said, "Can this be the Son of David?" But when the Pharisees heard it, they said, "It is only by Beelzebul, the ruler of the demons, that this fellow casts out the demons." He knew what they were thinking and said to them, "Every kingdom divided against itself is laid waste, and no city or house divided against itself will stand. If Satan casts out Satan, he is divided against himself; how then will his kingdom stand? If I cast out demons by Beelzebul, by whom do your own exorcists cast them out? Therefore they will be your judges. But if it is by the Spirit of God that I cast out demons, then the kingdom of God has come to you. Or how can one enter a strong man's house and plunder his property, without first tying up the strong man? Then indeed the house can be plundered. Whoever is not with me is against me, and whoever does not gather with me scatters. Therefore I tell you, people will be forgiven for every sin and blasphemy, but blasphemy against the Spirit will not be forgiven. Whoever speaks a word against the Son of Man will be forgiven, but whoever speaks against the Holy Spirit will not be forgiven, either in this age or in the age to come."

NOTES

FOR FURTHER READING MATTHEW 12:9-14

LECTIO DIVINA

hosanna

What is Jesus saying or doing in this passage?

What does this passage reveal to me about God's mercy?

In what area of my life do I need to hear this message of mercy?

We've made immense progress in the fields of psychiatry over the last hundred years. These advances, while bringing relief to people who struggle with mental illness, have also had the side effect of making Christians wonder what is meant when St. Matthew tells us that Jesus cast out demons from a demoniac.

The temptation for a rational, intellectual Christian of our era is to explain away demons simply as undiagnosed mental illness. The *Catechism of the Catholic Church*, however, distinguishes the two:

> Exorcism is directed at the expulsion of demons or to the liberation from demonic possession through the spiritual authority which Jesus entrusted to his Church. Illness, especially psychological illness, is a very different matter; treating this is the concern of medical science. (1673)

Holly is an atheist who considers me to be her "rational Christian friend." A while ago, she asked me my thoughts on an article about demonic influences on current events. The tone of her question was skeptical at best, and I found myself giving a very vague non-answer. I don't remember the article, and I don't remember my answer, but years later, I remember that I put my fear of appearing crazy above honesty.

If I believe in an infallible God and that Jesus was truly God, then I must believe that Jesus knew the difference between illness and possession. When he said, "But if it is by the Spirit of God that I cast out demons, then the kingdom of God has come to you" (Matthew 12:28), he was pointing to his own divinity, and not merely using the language of the day to explain away illness.

The spiritual realm, although unseen, is as real as the natural world, and it can neither be contained in nor denied by science. The *Catechism* teaches us that the spiritual world is real, and that it can influence the physical world. It also teaches us that angels are a "truth of the faith" (328), that we each have our own particular guardian angel (see 336), and that "demons are fallen angels who have freely refused to serve God and his plan" (414). We need not be afraid though, for Christ has already won the final victory over Satan and all sin! (For more on angels, demons, and the spiritual world, see the *Catechism*, 325-421.)

When I was younger, I did myself a disservice by limiting my faith in just that which I could see and hear and touch. Though I professed to believe in the supernatural world in the Creed at Mass, I was as guilty of this as my atheist friend Holly, albeit on a more subconscious level.

Do I believe that there is a spiritual battle to be won and that I have a part in it? Do I believe that through Jesus Christ, Holy Mother Church has the power to expel demons and protect the members of the body of Christ? The answer today is an unequivocal yes.

We, as soldiers of Jesus Christ, King of kings, however, can have the assurance that no other army in the history of the world has ever had: that our war is already won and our King is the victor.

How then do we protect ourselves from supernatural evil and play our God-given role in the spiritual battle around us?

First and foremost, we remain steadfast in the sacraments, primarily penance and Communion, as they provide us with actual grace with which to avoid sin and evil. We can also enlist the assistance of the guardian angel God has provided us. Make that angel your friend and confidant! The St. Michael Prayer is also a powerful prayer of protection. Finally, it's imperative that we seek the necessary assistance, whether medical or psychological help for mental illness or the guidance of a holy priest if we believe we need spiritual protection.

I've often thought about how I would discuss that long-ago article with Holly now, after having thought about her question for a decade. I'm still not sure exactly what I would say, but I would endeavor to be as true to Jesus' holy Scriptures as possible. The older I get, the more I realize that as Christians, we are called to a deep spiritual courage. This unseen battle could use some brave warriors.

In fact, I think our world is desperate for them.

Micaela Darr

OPEN YOUR BIBLE Matthew 13:54-58

He came to his hometown and began to teach the people in their synagogue, so that they were astounded and said, "Where did this man get this wisdom and these deeds of power? Is not this the carpenter's son? Is not his mother called Mary? And are not his brothers James and Joseph and Simon and Judas? And are not all his sisters with us? Where then did this man get all this?" And they took offense at him. But Jesus said to them, "Prophets are not without honor except in their own country and in their own house." And he did not do many deeds of power there, because of their unbelief.

NOTES

FOR FURTHER READING　　MATTHEW 13:44-50

LECTIO DIVINA

hosanna

What is Jesus saying or doing in this passage?

What does this passage reveal to me about God's mercy?

In what area of my life do I need to hear this message of mercy?

thursday of the fourth week of lent

Difficulty recognizing God is a recurring theme in the Bible: the burning bush for Moses, the small whisper for Elijah, the disciples unknowingly walking with the risen Christ on the road to Emmaus. Each time it takes God working on our behalf, out of his mercy, for people to recognize him. It also takes a bit of faith.

When the people in Jesus' hometown don't recognize him as the Messiah and instead ask, "Is not this the carpenter's son?," Jesus doesn't work to help them see. Instead, he rebukes them because of their lack of faith.

It's easy for us to hear this and think, this rebuke is for them, for those people who don't have faith in Christ. The people from his hometown don't recognize him for who he is because they are hard-hearted and blinded by their familiarity with him.

But when we look closer, we see it's really a rebuke of deep-seated problems of the human heart that drive out faith in all of us: pride and prejudice. The Gospel says they did see, and were amazed, by his wisdom and miraculous powers—things that elsewhere in the Gospels helped others to have faith in Jesus. But they couldn't accept his greatness because of their own pride. Jesus was a carpenter and came from a lower class than many people in his town. Pride pricked at them: who does he think he is? Prejudice blinded them: isn't his mother Mary? Where then did he get all this power? And they took offense at him.

Pride and prejudice lead us to make up our minds about people, about ourselves, and about God. And we don't even see how limited our perceptions are. As an experiment, think about what thoughts you've had about other people at church as you looked around. Anyone trying to advance in the spiritual life begins to notice that the ego— particularly the wounded ego—is the devil's most efficient way to separate us from God and each other. In our weaker moments we might see God working in other people's lives and think, why are they getting those gifts and I am not?

But God is magnanimous. His mercy and love are more than we can imagine. It takes the opposite of pride to see it. We need the humility of repentance and of our littleness to see the great things he can do through us and through the people around us. When Jesus could see that his townspeople didn't have this humility, he didn't work miracles there. What has he tried to do in us but couldn't because of our pride? Or our limited perceptions? Or our lack of faith?

Let's instead take Jesus' rebuke as an invitation to have an open mind about what God is doing. An invitation to have a deeper faith. We only need to look towards Mary and the saints to see what this looks like. Instead of pride, they embrace humility. Instead of prejudice, they lift others up and encourage people while emptying themselves.

St. Thérèse of Lisieux thought she could do nothing great except to love in small, tiny ways. St. John Bosco saw the hordes of poor boys who needed education and responded. St. Teresa of Calcutta didn't let the prejudices of a caste system keep her from showing the poor and the dying dignity. Seeing our own littleness, while seeing the greatness and potential in others, is a hallmark of holiness.

Imagine what would happen in our marriages, in our families, and in our communities if we strove to see God's image in others or the gifts he's given them or the magnanimity of how he works through them? We only need to think how wonderful it feels when others see these things in us to see what effect it would have.

Let's pray this Lent that we have the humility to recognize him in those around us, in all his magnanimity and mercy.

Katie Curtis

FRIDAY OF THE FOURTH WEEK OF LENT

OPEN YOUR BIBLE Matthew 14:22-33

Immediately he made the disciples get into the boat and go on ahead to the other side, while he dismissed the crowds. And after he had dismissed the crowds, he went up the mountain by himself to pray. When evening came, he was there alone, but by this time the boat, battered by the waves, was far from the land, for the wind was against them. And early in the morning he came walking toward them on the sea. But when the disciples saw him walking on the sea, they were terrified, saying, "It is a ghost!" And they cried out in fear. But immediately Jesus spoke to them and said, "Take heart, it is I; do not be afraid."

Peter answered him, "Lord, if it is you, command me to come to you on the water." He said, "Come." So Peter got out of the boat, started walking on the water, and came toward Jesus. But when he noticed the strong wind, he became frightened, and beginning to sink, he cried out, "Lord, save me!" Jesus immediately reached out his hand and caught him, saying to him, "You of little faith, why did you doubt?" When they got into the boat, the wind ceased. And those in the boat worshiped him, saying, "Truly you are the Son of God."

NOTES

FOR FURTHER READING MATTHEW 14:1-12

LECTIO DIVINA

hosanna

What is Jesus saying or doing in this passage?

What does this passage reveal to me about God's mercy?

In what area of my life do I need to hear this message of mercy?

Some years ago I was leading a retreat for high school seniors, encouraging them to live for Jesus and to get off the boat and let him show them how to walk on water. A key moment came when I led the kids through a meditation on today's passage. They closed their eyes and imagined themselves in this scene, the waves pounding, the apostles frantically bailing water from the storm-ravaged boat. Then Jesus comes walking toward them on the water and calls them.

After the meditation was over, one of the guys hung back to talk to me.

"How was your meditation?" I asked, hoping earnestly to start a meaningful conversation with this young man who generally preferred to keep things light.

"Yeah, it was good. You know, I was on this yacht, with all these beautiful women in bikinis. Champagne, hors d'oeuvres—I was having a pretty great time." I narrowly avoided rolling my eyes. As usual, it seemed, he was making light of things.

"And, uh . . . and then Jesus called my name."

Suddenly he was serious. Looking straight in my eyes as his buddy (who'd been grinning smugly at his earlier description) realized that he wasn't messing around and took off.

"He did?"

"Yeah. Yeah, he did. Looked right in my eyes and called my name."

"So what did you do?"

"I turned my back on him."

"You turned your back on Jesus?"

"Yeah. He called my name and he looked into my eyes and I turned my back and walked away."

"Because you were afraid you'd sink?"

"No," he said. "I knew I wouldn't sink. I was afraid I wouldn't be happy."

I felt like I'd been hit—it was so raw and pained and honest. He trusted that God could raise the dead and make ordinary guys walk on water. But he didn't trust God to make him happy. He knew God's power but he didn't know his love.

I wonder if Peter had a similar fear. He knew what Jesus was capable of, after all, but as he stepped off the boat and the roar of the wind intensified, as his brother shouted for him to stop being an idiot, perhaps, and get back on the boat, as the danger of following Jesus suddenly became so much more apparent, did he forget God's love?

I know you and I do. We make some decision to live for Jesus, to make a financial sacrifice or choose a certain career or end a relationship or welcome another child, and suddenly the sound of the waves drowns out the sound of his voice. We see all the ways things could go wrong, and while we might trust that we'll be okay and that he'll save us from drowning, we worry that we won't be happy.

So Peter fell. And so do we. Even if we don't turn our backs on Jesus, we become resentful or halfhearted. We take our eyes off him and begin to sink.

Thank God for that. Because when we feel the water closing over us, it's then that we finally fix our eyes on him again and call out his name. It's then that he grasps our hand, lifts us up, and looks into our eyes with the world's deepest love. It's then that we begin to trust that he loves us—not as a reward for unflappable faith but as a consolation when we've fallen.

If you've fallen, even if you've just "abandoned the love you had at first" (Revelation 2:4), cry out his name. So often we turn from the Lord because we don't trust that he loves us. We don't believe that he wants us to be happy. But when we reach out to him in our brokenness, we begin to see his love in a way that we never did when we were walking blithely and blindly in his ways. Where mercy is, grace abounds. Get off the boat.

Meg Hunter-Kilmer

SELAH

PAUSE PRAYER PRAISE REST

As an apple tree among the trees of the wood, / so is my beloved among young men. / With great delight I sat in his shadow, / and his fruit was sweet to my taste. / He brought me to the banqueting house, and his intention toward me was love.

Song of Solomon 2:3-4

Check in.

TODAY'S DATE	PLACE OF PEACE:
_____ | ___ | ___	_____

I'M FEELING

- ○ happy
- ○ excited
- ○ joyful

- ○ anxious
- ○ upset
- ○ tired

- ○ annoyed
- ○ angry
- ○ sad

- ○ grateful
- ○ confused
- ○ calm

- ○ _____
- ○ _____
- ○ _____

Outside my window:

Small successes:

Giving thanks for:

Working on my heart:

Listening to:

In my prayers:

Hope for next week:

"Rejoice and be glad, for your reward is great in heaven."

MATTHEW 5:12

scripture memory

MATTHEW 5:11-12

"Blessed are you when people revile you
and persecute you and utter
all kinds of evil against you
falsely on my account.
Rejoice and be glad, for your reward is great in heaven,
for in the same way they persecuted the prophets
who were before you."

I will practice Scripture memory by:
○ Praying
○ Writing
○ Speaking
○ Reading
○ Other: _____

OPEN YOUR BIBLE Matthew 16:24-28

Then Jesus told his disciples, "If any want to become my followers, let them deny themselves and take up their cross and follow me. For those who want to save their life will lose it, and those who lose their life for my sake will find it. For what will it profit them if they gain the whole world but forfeit their life? Or what will they give in return for their life?

"For the Son of Man is to come with his angels in the glory of his Father, and then he will repay everyone for what has been done. Truly I tell you, there are some standing here who will not taste death before they see the Son of Man coming in his kingdom."

NOTES

FOR FURTHER READING MATTHEW 15:10-20

LECTIO DIVINA

hosanna

What is Jesus saying or doing in this passage?

What does this passage reveal to me about God's mercy?

In what area of my life do I need to hear this message of mercy?

monday of the fifth week of lent

I want to be a disciple of Christ. In fact, if asked, I'd likely say that I already am. And yet, when I'm faced with what Jesus specifically requested of his followers, I have to pause and wonder if I'm really doing as he asks.

The past few years of my life have undoubtedly been the most tumultuous and suffering-filled yet. And while I've often initially fought and whined in response to the crosses that have come my way, I have also tried my best to bear them. So it's tempting to pat myself on the back and conclude that I am indeed living as a disciple of Christ.

But Jesus isn't merely asking us to bear the crosses we're given: he's calling us to take up a specific cross. He's calling us to action, not just acceptance. We are indeed called to unite our suffering with his and doing so allows us to take part in the story of redemption in an incredible way. Yet, we are also called to choose the cross of discipleship—to follow him in a radical way despite the hardships that doing so will bring.

During his time on earth, Jesus told his disciples that following him necessitated an acceptance of death in the most painful and humiliating way. That reality was a large part of what their cross of discipleship would entail. For some Christians today, that is still true, and we are all called to accept that death may be a consequence of following Christ.

But for most of us, the pain and humiliation of discipleship will come in less dramatic or obvious ways. We might lose a dear friendship, relationship, or job because we live our faith out loud. We might suffer physical or mental exhaustion as we choose to serve others over ourselves. We might struggle to let go of the comforts the world tells us we deserve. And, in one way or another, we will all experience the pain of letting go of our plans and expectations for how our lives should turn out.

While the world continuously tells us to follow our heart and to be who we want to be, it is Christ's heart we are meant to follow, and God's beautiful version of who we are meant to be that we should strive to become. At times, this will necessitate the denial of our ambitions, desires, and inclinations, but ultimately it will also save our lives.

I've suffered and carried crosses, and I know that you have too. But this Lent, let's ask ourselves if we've chosen to take up the cross of discipleship too. And let us repent for the ways we have not, knowing that God's mercy is new every day.

Making the daily choice to be a disciple of Christ can seem overwhelming. But let us not lose hope or miss what else Jesus said, which is that we are to follow him. Because this reminds us that he has gone before us, and that when we share in his cross, we also share in the joy of his glorious resurrection.

Allison McGinley

TUESDAY OF THE FIFTH WEEK OF LENT

OPEN YOUR BIBLE

Matthew 17:1-13

Six days later, Jesus took with him Peter and James and his brother John and led them up a high mountain, by themselves. And he was transfigured before them, and his face shone like the sun, and his clothes became dazzling white. Suddenly there appeared to them Moses and Elijah, talking with him. Then Peter said to Jesus, "Lord, it is good for us to be here; if you wish, I will make three dwellings here, one for you, one for Moses, and one for Elijah." While he was still speaking, suddenly a bright cloud overshadowed them, and from the cloud a voice said, "This is my Son, the Beloved; with him I am well pleased; listen to him!" When the disciples heard this, they fell to the ground and were overcome by fear. But Jesus came and touched them, saying, "Get up and do not be afraid." And when they looked up, they saw no one except Jesus himself alone.

As they were coming down the mountain, Jesus ordered them, "Tell no one about the vision until after the Son of Man has been raised from the dead." And the disciples asked him, "Why, then, do the scribes say that Elijah must come first?" He replied, "Elijah is indeed coming and will restore all things; but I tell you that Elijah has already come, and they did not recognize him, but they did to him whatever they pleased. So also the Son of Man is about to suffer at their hands." Then the disciples understood that he was speaking to them about John the Baptist.

NOTES

FOR FURTHER READING MATTHEW 17:22-27

LECTIO DIVINA

hosanna

What is Jesus saying or doing in this passage?

What does this passage reveal to me about God's mercy?

In what area of my life do I need to hear this message of mercy?

While I was a sophomore at Boston College, my dad passed away suddenly a few weeks before Christmas. He had been burning a pile of leaves at our family's home in New Hampshire. The smoke triggered an asthma attack, which then triggered a heart attack. He was 59.

The Jesuits at BC held Mass every day, almost every hour, in an old gothic cathedral on campus. I stuck close to it as I grieved the rest of that year, and when I returned my junior year, it continued to be a solace to me. Jesus in the Eucharist, the ultimate comforter.

My plan had been to go abroad my junior year to the London School of Economics, influenced by my dad who had been an economics major at Notre Dame. But I wasn't sure if I still wanted to go after everything that had happened. Grief still clung to the peripheral vision of my days, and I wasn't sure it was the best time to be away from support in a new city. I prayed for discernment as I went ahead and filled out the forms to attend, and before I knew it, I was accepted and the funding was arranged, and it was time to get a passport.

I went to Mass on a crisp fall morning in the old chapel with the iron door that creaks as you enter, the walls of medieval stone and the stained glass windows glowing like jewels. I prayed hard after Communion about the trip, and when I finished praying, I got up and walked out to Commonwealth Avenue and down the block to a convenience store that took passport pictures.

When I got to the store to take the photo, it was fewer than ten minutes after I had received Communion. The clerk stepped out from behind the counter and over to where the camera was set up for pictures, and gestured at me to sit down. He took the picture, then pulled out the photo and stared at it.

"Hmm . . . that's weird. Must be ghosts," he said.

He handed me the picture, and there in the center of my chest, where the Eucharist I had just received would physically have been, was a glowing bright light. Over my shoulder was another glowing light, and I can't remember how, but I knew it was an angel keeping Christ company—maybe my guardian angel.

I was so shocked that I barely noticed that as I sat down for another photo, the clerk threw that one in the trash. He took another photo that would become my passport picture, and though my face beamed pure joy, there were no bright lights.

After Jesus brought Peter, James, and John to the top of the mountain and revealed to them his glory, the disciples received strength to endure their mission and their own deaths. Some speculate it even gave Jesus the strength to complete his mission on the cross. The *Catechism* states,

> Christ's Transfiguration aims at strengthening the apostles' faith in anticipation of his Passion: the ascent onto the "high mountain" prepares for the ascent to Calvary. Christ, Head of the Church, manifests what his Body contains and radiates in the sacraments: "the hope of glory." (568)

I didn't need to keep that photo or to tell anyone about it. I did go abroad, and it was a wonderful, healing experience that and allowed me the space to feel my grief without the usual distractions.

The moment I saw the bright light in my chest, when Jesus made manifest what his Body contains and radiates in the sacraments, I felt his amazing mercy, and my faith was strengthened to believe that anything is possible with God. Jesus had already been comforting me and strengthening my faith all along, with every Eucharist, even without that photo, but I am not sure I would have felt so prepared for my journey or would have left so confident or so filled with hope without it. That photo was like a grain of sand, a pinprick compared to the transfiguration. I can only imagine what faith and hope hearing the Father's voice, and seeing the fullness of Christ's glory, offered the apostles.

Katie Curtis

WEDNESDAY OF THE FIFTH WEEK OF LENT

OPEN YOUR BIBLE Matthew 18:6-9

"If any of you put a stumbling block before one of these little ones who believe in me, it would be better for you if a great millstone were fastened around your neck and you were drowned in the depth of the sea. Woe to the world because of stumbling blocks! Occasions for stumbling are bound to come, but woe to the one by whom the stumbling block comes!

"If your hand or your foot causes you to stumble, cut it off and throw it away; it is better for you to enter life maimed or lame than to have two hands or two feet and to be thrown into the eternal fire. And if your eye causes you to stumble, tear it out and throw it away; it is better for you to enter life with one eye than to have two eyes and to be thrown into the hell of fire."

NOTES

FOR FURTHER READING MATTHEW 18:15-22

LECTIO DIVINA

hosanna

What is Jesus saying or doing in this passage?

What does this passage reveal to me about God's mercy?

In what area of my life do I need to hear this message of mercy?

When I was in college studying theology and it was highly likely that many of us sitting at the desks would be going on to work in ministry, the professor, one of the most brilliant religious sisters I've known, would often reference the millstone. And we knew what she meant. This passage from Matthew is one of the most sobering and direct of Jesus' words to the disciples. In the body of Christ, we are culpable if we knowingly lead another away from the truth and into sin. We're even more culpable if we are in a position of authority. Jesus gives no equivocation about the gravity of leading one of his little ones into sin (scandal) as well as the abhorrence of our own sin. His words stand in stark and almost chilling contrast to a modern world that wants to minimize or even completely negate the idea of sin, guilt, culpability, and hell. It's tempting to want to gloss over this passage or try to play with the words to get them to mean something we are more comfortable with.

There's something insidious about sin. The infection grows where it is allowed room. Sin begets sin. When we become attached to a sin, our wills are weakened and we are more likely to get even sicker. When we are anxious to soothe a throbbing conscience, we often want to let the infection spread through rationalization and even encouragement of others in the same behavior. Sin begets sin.

Christ's way stops that cycle in its tracks. The antidote of grace is the only way to stop the infection from spreading. In our own life, he tells us to "cut it off" and "tear it out" (Matthew 18:8, 9). We are to be ruthless in rooting out sin from our own hearts. But the passage shows that our response to the sins of others must be different. When we respond to sin with more sin—judgment, participation, anger, gossip, scandal, and more—the situation only gets worse and the body sicker. It is when we meet sin with mercy, with the way of Christ, that true healing is possible.

Christ's way is far from our natural inclinations and often beyond our human understanding. His way is foolishness to the world. While we know that we are not called to literally cut off the hand that lead us to sin, Jesus uses that metaphor to make absolutely clear how seriously we must take our sin. It's probably not going to feel good to root it out. Is there something the Lord is asking me to make a clean break with—a relationship, addiction, position, job, or device? Am I somehow drawing others away from Christ? The *Catechism* tells us that "scandal is an attitude or behavior which leads another to do evil. The person who gives scandal becomes his neighbor's tempter" (2284). It goes on to say that that "scandal can be provoked by laws or institutions, by fashion or opinion" (2286).

It's easy to think of scandal as something huge and newsworthy. But when we read the full definition, it can be sobering to admit how often we might be participating in it. Have I in some way become a stumbling block for others? Do I water down the truth so I don't have to be embarrassed or unfriended? Do my speech, my writing, and my lifestyle reflect someone who loves and imitates Christ? Contrary to pop theology, in the body of Christ, we are culpable for how we lead— or don't lead—others to him. Are there ways that I am becoming a source of temptation to my family, friends, neighbors, or strangers?

What about when I am confronted with the sin of others? Later in Matthew 18, Christ guides the apostles in how to address this very thing. We are to proceed cautiously, through relationship and through relentless mercy, forgiving seventy-seven times. To be clear, this isn't the same as excusing a sin or tolerating evil. It's simply modeling our mercy after his. How often do we get that backwards? How often are we full of mercy and rationalization towards our own sin yet ruthless when we judge the sins of others? Does my response to sin and scandal only continue the cycle? Lord, help me to resist the pull to meet sin with sin and respond instead with the foolishness of mercy—the mercy with which you have met mine.

Mary Haseltine

THURSDAY OF THE FIFTH WEEK OF LENT

OPEN YOUR BIBLE ▶ Matthew 19:16-30

Then someone came to him and said, "Teacher, what good deed must I do to have eternal life?" And he said to him, "Why do you ask me about what is good? There is only one who is good. If you wish to enter into life, keep the commandments." He said to him, "Which ones?" And Jesus said, "You shall not murder; You shall not commit adultery; You shall not steal; You shall not bear false witness; Honor your father and mother; also, You shall love your neighbor as yourself." The young man said to him, "I have kept all these; what do I still lack?" Jesus said to him, "If you wish to be perfect, go, sell your possessions, and give the money to the poor, and you will have treasure in heaven; then come, follow me." When the young man heard this word, he went away grieving, for he had many possessions.

Then Jesus said to his disciples, "Truly I tell you, it will be hard for a rich person to enter the kingdom of heaven. Again I tell you, it is easier for a camel to go through the eye of a needle than for someone who is rich to enter the kingdom of God." When the disciples heard this, they were greatly astounded and said, "Then who can be saved?" But Jesus looked at them and said, "For mortals it is impossible, but for God all things are possible."

Then Peter said in reply, "Look, we have left everything and followed you. What then will we have?" Jesus said to them, "Truly I tell you, at the renewal of all things, when the Son of Man is seated on the throne of his glory, you who have followed me will also sit on twelve thrones, judging the twelve tribes of Israel. And everyone who has left houses or brothers or sisters or father or mother or children or fields, for my name's sake, will receive a hundredfold, and will inherit eternal life. But many who are first will be last, and the last will be first."

FOR FURTHER READING ▶ MATTHEW 20:20-28

LECTIO DIVINA

hosanna

What is Jesus saying or doing in this passage?

What does this passage reveal to me about God's mercy?

In what area of my life do I need to hear this message of mercy?

The story of Jesus and the rich man seems perfect for Lent—the time when we're called to strip ourselves of the things that keep us from Jesus. But it's also a story that most people can probably recite in their sleep. As I reread it in preparation for writing this essay, a few things jumped out at me.

The rich man, we are told, went away from his encounter with Jesus "grieving" (verse 22). Think about that—not just sad, but grieving. He had so many things weighing him down and keeping him from following Jesus that it created in him the sort of sadness we generally associate with death.

Why? Probably because he knew that Jesus was being serious. Jesus wasn't asking the rich man to follow him into some trendy form of minimalism for the fun of it. He was really telling the rich man that he had to do these things in order to have eternal life, and that was a huge step outside of his comfort zone. The rich man was so ensconced in his nest of wealth and possessions that he couldn't stand to give them up for any reason. That's some serious attachment to the materially good life.

And this is where we should pause. How are we doing in the "stuff" sweepstakes? As twenty-first century Westerners, we have a lot of stuff. And it's nice stuff. These things are not inherently bad, but if we're not careful, they can suffocate us and disconnect us. Possessions are not the be-all end-all. Human beings were created for more than rushing around to get the newest iPad, an upgraded car, or another stamp in our passports. Our hearts crave the eternal things—things that really give life, and Jesus knows that. He told us this just a few chapters ago:

> "Do not store up for yourselves treasures on earth, where
> moth and rust consume and where thieves break in and steal;
> but store up for yourselves treasures in heaven, where neither

moth nor rust consumes and where thieves do not break in and steal. For where your treasure is, there your heart will be also." (Matthew 6:19-21)

Where our treasure is, there will our heart be also. If our treasure is here on earth, then we have a problem. Because that sort of wealth? It doesn't last.

This doesn't mean that possessions are bad. Everyone, even cloistered nuns, needs a certain number of things. We're not all going to hell because we have laptops and indoor plumbing and two pairs of jeans. The important thing is that we cultivate a spirit of detachment. If the idea of having your car door nicked sends you into a panic, then you're not detached from your car. It's owning you. And that's the rich man's problem.

Do we have more money in the bank than we can possibly spend, because we want to be "secure"? Do we panic at the idea of giving anything away because we might need it later? We all know we can't take our things with us, but do our lives reflect what we intellectually know?

At the end of this passage, Peter asks Jesus a very human question. He's given up everything to follow Jesus, and he wants to know what he's going to get for it. He's left his wife and he's here following Jesus—but is Jesus really worthy of his trust?

And what does Jesus say? Peter, and everyone else who left everything to follow Jesus, all through the centuries, will get back a hundredfold. They will get more than they had before. We can never be more generous than God. But we can't begrudge what we've given God either. We can't keep looking back at what we've given up to follow Jesus (see Luke 9:62). We have to trust that Jesus is going to take care of us, because he is. His care for us is splashed all over the pages of the Gospel.

Can you—do you—trust Jesus that much?

Emily DeArdo

FRIDAY OF THE FIFTH WEEK OF LENT

OPEN YOUR BIBLE Matthew 21:1-11

When they had come near Jerusalem and had reached Bethphage, at the Mount of Olives, Jesus sent two disciples, saying to them, "Go into the village ahead of you, and immediately you will find a donkey tied, and a colt with her; untie them and bring them to me. If anyone says anything to you, just say this, 'The Lord needs them.' And he will send them immediately." This took place to fulfill what had been spoken through the prophet, saying,

> "Tell the daughter of Zion,
> Look, your king is coming to you,
>   humble, and mounted on a donkey,
>   and on a colt, the foal of a donkey."

The disciples went and did as Jesus had directed them; they brought the donkey and the colt, and put their cloaks on them, and he sat on them. A very large crowd spread their cloaks on the road, and others cut branches from the trees and spread them on the road. The crowds that went ahead of him and that followed were shouting,

> "Hosanna to the Son of David!
>   Blessed is the one who comes in the name of the Lord!
> Hosanna in the highest heaven!"

When he entered Jerusalem, the whole city was in turmoil, asking, "Who is this?" The crowds were saying, "This is the prophet Jesus from Nazareth in Galilee."

FOR FURTHER READING   MATTHEW 21:12-17
MATTHEW 22:1-14

LECTIO DIVINA

hosanna

What is Jesus saying or doing in this passage?

What does this passage reveal to me about God's mercy?

In what area of my life do I need to hear this message of mercy?

One of the most beautiful Masses of the year, Palm Sunday, is coming up this weekend. The church and the congregation will be decked out in red, the palm fronds a soft olive green as we lift them high to welcome the King of kings into Jerusalem.

Yet the Scripture always makes me ache a little. The people of Jerusalem were so close to doing the right thing! They welcomed Jesus with praise and worship, laying their very clothes in the dust so that his humble donkey wouldn't get dirty.

> "Hosanna to the Son of David!
> Blessed is the one who comes in the name of the Lord!
> Hosanna in the highest heaven!" (Matthew 21:9)

Hosanna is a Hebrew word meaning both "long live" and "save us." The Israelites had been waiting thousands of years for their Messiah to come. From him they expected kingly glory ("long live") and deliverance ("save us").

On that day in Jerusalem, many Hebrews saw and identified Jesus Christ as their Messiah, and they poured all their long years—indeed, generations—of waiting into praise for him. He didn't come simply for glory, however, but to chastise them and lead them away from sin so they could experience true freedom. We see this in the next passages when he cleanses the temple:

> Then Jesus entered the temple and drove out all who were selling and buying in the temple, and he overturned the tables of the money changers and the seats of those who sold doves. (Matthew 21:12)

I remember once, while pregnant with my sixth child, I stayed home from Mass due to illness. In order to assuage my guilt (I never know if I'm "sick enough") I decided to pray quietly while the rest of my family was gone. In the middle of my Divine Mercy chaplet, I had such a comforting sense of Jesus' presence. When I opened my eyes, I felt like I could see a shimmer of something there, as though if only my eyes could focus well enough, I would be able to see my True Love.

Alas, two weeks later, I was in the depths of despair over my late pregnancy woes. I felt sure God didn't hear me, see me, or love me at all. Why did I have to suffer these incredible pains and humiliations? Was there even a God at all?

I dare say we all have those spiritual highs and lows. We have moments when we welcome Jesus Christ into our lives with praise and worship. We proclaim his goodness and we meekly lay our cloaks down before him. In those ecstatic moments, we cannot imagine a low point.

And yet, the low points always come. Jesus comes into our lives and brings chastisement, or at the very least allows us to suffer for our own sanctification. He cleanses our temple and as our sins are made visible, oftentimes this makes us feel indignant, like the Pharisees in the temple of Jerusalem.

That was how I felt too in those tumultuously hormonal moments of late pregnancy. Never mind, Lord. This is too hard. How dare you ask more of me? I'll go back to life before the sanctification, but thanks anyway.

There was a little voice inside that reminded me of that wonderful Divine Mercy Chaplet, though. It reminded me of that moment when I could nearly see Jesus, when I was completely sure of the existence of the King of the universe and of his love and care for me. Could I draw myself back to that moment of certainty?

What if, in those moments of indignation, we hearken back to our own personal Palm Sunday in Jerusalem? What if we remember, in moments of desolation, the joy and peace and wonder it brings us to worship our Lord with all our heart? Can we pray our Hosanna through every moment, being assured that even when we feel "low," God's kingship is as true as it ever was?

Micaela Darr

SELAH

PAUSE
PRAYER
PRAISE
REST

Let my prayer be counted
as incense before you,
and the lifting up of my hands
as an evening sacrifice.

Psalm 141:2

Check in.

TODAY'S DATE

PLACE OF PEACE:

I'M FEELING

- ○ happy
- ○ excited
- ○ joyful

- ○ anxious
- ○ upset
- ○ tired

- ○ annoyed
- ○ angry
- ○ sad

- ○ grateful
- ○ confused
- ○ calm

- ○ _____
- ○ _____
- ○ _____

Outside my window:

Working on my heart:

Small successes:

Listening to:

In my prayers:

Giving thanks for:

Hope for next week:

"Blessed is the one who comes in the name of the Lord!" "Hosanna in the highest heaven!"

MATTHEW 21:9

scripture memory

MATTHEW 21:9

The crowds that went ahead of him
and that followed were shouting,

"Hosanna to the Son of David!
Blessed is the one who comes in the name of the Lord!
Hosanna in the highest heaven!"

I will practice Scripture memory by:
- ○ Praying
- ○ Writing
- ○ Speaking
- ○ Reading
- ○ Other: _____

MONDAY OF HOLY WEEK

OPEN YOUR BIBLE Matthew 22:34-40

When the Pharisees heard that he had silenced the Sadducees, they gathered together, and one of them, a lawyer, asked him a question to test him. "Teacher, which commandment in the law is the greatest?" He said to him, "'You shall love the Lord your God with all your heart, and with all your soul, and with all your mind.' This is the greatest and first commandment. And a second is like it: 'You shall love your neighbor as yourself.' On these two commandments hang all the law and the prophets."

NOTES

FOR FURTHER READING MATTHEW 23

LECTIO DIVINA

hosanna

What is Jesus saying or doing in this passage?

What does this passage reveal to me about God's mercy?

In what area of my life do I need to hear this message of mercy?

monday of holy week

The two great commandments stand side by side, spoken by our Lord in answer to the Pharisees' attempt to set a trap for him. Interestingly, the more the religious lawmakers complicate their plans to trip up Jesus, the more clearly Jesus is able to distill the gospel message. Love God. Love others. Oh, and also, a far too often overlooked third section: Love yourself. Love your neighbor as yourself he says. I hardly think he means to admonish us for self-love here, because how would that inspire us to love our neighbors well? Jesus genuinely wants us to understand that spiritual love hinges on our ability to value ourselves as gift—we gift ourselves, heart, soul, and strength to God, and we gift ourselves to our neighbor.

When I find myself lagging in my prayer and Scripture study habits, I have learned that the first thing I need to do is a shame check. What has me feeling like I need to hide from God, echoing the first shame of our first parents in the Garden of Eden? For me, many times it is not simply a feeling of guilt for something sinful I have done that sends me into the shame spiral. Most often, it is a cumulative effect of a long history of self-criticism which leads to self-loathing, a feeling that I am not good enough for God and I do not want to be seen by an all-loving Father because I don't deserve that kind of love. And I am hardly capable of willing the best for someone else when I am determined to give myself the worst.

This Christmas, my five sons stood proudly before me and handed me a simple wooden box they had painted my favorite turquoise color. On it were the current versions of their signatures, and tucked inside were handwritten notes that recounted the reasons they love me.

Yes, I cried. And oh, the number of times I have revisited that box in the days since Christmas, reminding myself, in the moments when I feel less than loveable, how deeply loved I am. That box also stands as a reminder to me of God's love for me. These children are an undeserved gift; the daily blessings of life with them are my witness that the hand of a loving Father is ever-present. I am overwhelmed with a rush of gratitude that compels me to offer him love in return. And in remembering how loved I am, I am able to offer myself some compassion and love too.

Love notes. Such a simple gesture from the hands of young hearts with such a profound effect. But the truth is, my every day is filled with love notes from God. He has left them scrawled across the pages of Scripture, written in the pink sunset, glistening on a bed of fresh snow, and in the eyes of these boys who love me so well. If I just live with a heart tuned to love, shame melts away, and I see the gift of myself I have been given by the hand of a loving Father. Suddenly I am scribbling love notes back to him in the prayers on my lips and the work of my hands and the words I speak to others. The lens of love becomes the way I see the world, and the world is easy to love through his eyes.

Perhaps it is as simple as this distilled gospel makes it after all. Let God love you—that is the first step. And maybe the hardest. But look around. See the love notes from him written across your life. Take notice. Be overwhelmed. When you remember that you have been gifted Love himself and he has made you a gift worth giving, you will have love to give in abundance.

Colleen Connell

TUESDAY OF HOLY WEEK

OPEN YOUR BIBLE Matthew 24:9-14

"Then they will hand you over to be tortured and will put you to death, and you will be hated by all nations because of my name. Then many will fall away, and they will betray one another and hate one another. And many false prophets will arise and lead many astray. And because of the increase of lawlessness, the love of many will grow cold. But the one who endures to the end will be saved. And this good news of the kingdom will be proclaimed throughout the world, as a testimony to all the nations; and then the end will come."

NOTES

FOR FURTHER READING   MATTHEW 24:15-28
MATTHEW 24:36-44

LECTIO DIVINA

hosanna

What is Jesus saying or doing in this passage?

What does this passage reveal to me about God's mercy?

In what area of my life do I need to hear this message of mercy?

There were moments when I thought the end times sounded rather glorious and dramatic. I could see myself boldly standing in defiance of worldly powers that were trying to force me to renounce Christ. In those imaginings I would (of course!) stand firm in my faith, partaking in a climactic and thrilling martyrdom mimicking that of the saints that I had read about in so many books. It wasn't until I grew older (and perhaps a bit more humble) that I realized that if I was weak in denying myself and my own wants and comfort in little things, how in the world did I dare to think I'd be able to endure some heroic martyrdom? Those saints who had been martyred didn't fulfill that call in a vacuum. They had trained themselves in a thousand normal everyday martyrdoms so that they could endure the ultimate one. And here I was struggling to "only" eat two snacks and a light meal on Ash Wednesday!

But there have also been times where I teetered to the other end of the spectrum and experienced the idea of an Armageddon as paralyzing. The ideas presented in Scripture, when taken literally, are more than a bit terrifying, not to mention all the doomsday prophesies and interpretations resulting from them that can be so easy to get pulled into. Is my soul ready? Will I be part of the elect or will I be one of those spit out of his mouth (see Revelation 3:16)? What about my children? While those passages are good to wrestle with, it is easy to fall into fear or even despair on one end or, perhaps as a sort of defense mechanism, scramble to the other, rejecting and writing it all off as nonsense.

Faithful Scripture scholars, though, will point out that the end times are not just to be interpreted as some isolated far-off moment to be predicted in the future, though there is that element to be sure. The end times are also right now. We are dwelling in the midst of the end of the ages. "With the Lord one day is as a thousand years, and a thousand years are like one day," 2 Peter 3:8 tells us. Christ came, he saved, and he is still in the process of renewing all the world in him through the grace of the paschal mystery. So when we read the words of Christ in these passages, we can see them as signs pointing to an immediate end of the world, but we can also view them as signs marking today, right now.

We will see people hated because of him now. We will see betrayal, wickedness, people falling away, and love growing cold now. We will see desolating sacrilege, false prophets, and tribulation now. These things can and should sadden us and grieve us and prompt us to discern wisely, pray hard, and make reparations as we can, but none of these things should shock us. We are in the midst of the end of the age.

The Christian heart is not a fretful one. It is not one that is easily shaken. It is one that throws itself at the foot of his cross and becomes renewed in the mercy and hope that only Christ can give. But the Christian heart is also not a complacent one. It is one that prepares itself for tribulation, and when it comes, remains steadfast in faith. In some respects, my job isn't to fret about the ultimate end times, but simply to be prepared right now.

We are guaranteed an end. Whether we make it to the end of the world or to the end of our earthly life, Christ implores us to be prepared. His mercy is abundant and he longs to pour it out upon us. Because of that, the opportunities he gives us to prepare are many. We can prepare ourselves for such trials by rooting ourselves in the Word, through fervent prayer, fasting, frequenting the sacraments, and through love. We can allow the signs of the times around us right now, rather than to prompt us toward cynicism or despair, to prompt us in love to pray for an even greater outpouring of his Precious Blood upon all. And if we are prepared and endure? Oh, what hope we can have! Then we can bear these end days looking forward in steady joy and anticipation, rather than presumption or panic, to his coming again in glory.

Mary Haseltine

WEDNESDAY OF HOLY WEEK

OPEN YOUR BIBLE Matthew 25:31-46

"When the Son of Man comes in his glory, and all the angels with him, then he will sit on the throne of his glory. All the nations will be gathered before him, and he will separate people one from another as a shepherd separates the sheep from the goats, and he will put the sheep at his right hand and the goats at the left. Then the king will say to those at his right hand, 'Come, you that are blessed by my Father, inherit the kingdom prepared for you from the foundation of the world; for I was hungry and you gave me food, I was thirsty and you gave me something to drink, I was a stranger and you welcomed me, I was naked and you gave me clothing, I was sick and you took care of me, I was in prison and you visited me.' Then the righteous will answer him, 'Lord, when was it that we saw you hungry and gave you food, or thirsty and gave you something to drink? And when was it that we saw you a stranger and welcomed you, or naked and gave you clothing? And when was it that we saw you sick or in prison and visited you?' And the king will answer them, 'Truly I tell you, just as you did it to one of the least of these who are members of my family, you did it to me.' Then he will say to those at his left hand, 'You that are accursed, depart from me into the eternal fire prepared for the devil and his angels; for I was hungry and you gave me no food, I was thirsty and you gave me nothing to drink, I was a stranger and you did not welcome me, naked and you did not give me clothing, sick and in prison and you did not visit me.' Then they also will answer, 'Lord, when was it that we saw you hungry or thirsty or a stranger or naked or sick or in prison, and did not take care of you?' Then he will answer them, 'Truly I tell you, just as you did not do it to one of the least of these, you did not do it to me.' And these will go away into eternal punishment, but the righteous into eternal life."

FOR FURTHER READING MATTHEW 25:1-30

LECTIO DIVINA

hosanna

What is Jesus saying or doing in this passage?

What does this passage reveal to me about God's mercy?

In what area of my life do I need to hear this message of mercy?

wednesday of holy week

Over twenty years later, I still remember the day so vividly. There I was, nineteen years old, sitting at a soup kitchen outside of San Diego. My parents had decided to spend the holiday with close family friends in California, and they had arranged for us to serve the less fortunate on Christmas morning. So off we went, my Hindu parents, Jewish "godparents," and me.

When we arrived, I was tasked with handing out presents to the children along with a young Marine who had also chosen to serve that morning. His name was Elijah, and he was celebrating his twenty-first birthday. Until that moment, I had never met anyone who would choose to celebrate a twenty-first birthday serving the poor instead of being served copious amounts of alcohol.

Elijah shared that had he stayed on base, he would in fact have been pressured to celebrate as was customary among my crowd—drunken revelry. Since he was a devout Baptist, that was not his scene. Instead, he wanted to honor his Savior by serving those who had nothing. He explained that he had been blessed so richly and he wanted to pour that out on others.

I had read only a little of Scripture, but these verses from Matthew were among them. Serving alongside Elijah that morning, the words took on life as they embedded themselves in my heart. It was Jesus we served that day. It was his light in the eyes of the children who received the gifts we gave. It was his gratitude in the faces of those we fed and spent lunch alongside. That day, I had my first tangible encounter with the person of Jesus Christ.

As the years have gone by, these verses have come to mean so much more to me. The deeper I understand my own need for Christ and my own brokenness and humanity, the more I begin to grasp the pure gift of his mercy. Sisters, we cannot comprehend the depth of God's mercy without first claiming our own poverty. I fought for so long to be "fine." I wasn't fine. I used alcohol to cope with anxiety and loneliness. I was so desperate to feel loved that I chased after whatever fleeting attention I could grab. This only led to more anxiety and loneliness. Though on the surface everything seemed "fine," I ended up in a vicious cycle that left me broken time and time again.

I went to confession but I glossed over the sins I was embarrassed about, minimizing their effect on me. I was hiding from God. It wasn't until the night I finally surrendered everything to Jesus, sobbing on my couch desperate to be set free from my self-inflicted prisons, that I was flooded with the sure knowledge of his mercy and love. I know my life could look so much different today if not for his grace.

Aside from being the only description of the judgment of the nations in Scripture, these verses from Matthew tell a story of love and mercy poured out. St. Teresa of Calcutta used to say that Christ comes to us in distressing disguise. We—each of us—are that distressing disguise. In our poverty and hunger, Christ is there. In our shame and our prisons, Christ is there. When we know what Jesus has done for us in our distress, we are called to pour out that mercy onto others without judgment. We are called to recognize Jesus in those who are struggling and to share with them the overflowing love of Christ who lives in us.

I invite you to contemplate your own poverty as you read these verses. Where do you most need Christ to quench your thirst or to free you? How have you ignored someone in need? Allow Jesus to flood you with his mercy, and share that gift of mercy with another this season.

Rakhi McCormick

TRI
DU
UM

• • •

TRIDUUM

• • •

Holy Thursday
*While they were eating, Jesus took a loaf of bread,
and after blessing it he broke it,
gave it to the disciples, and said,
"Take, eat; this is my body."*

Matthew 26:26

Good Friday
*Then Jesus cried again with a loud voice
and breathed his last.*

Matthew 27:50

Holy Saturday
*So they went with the guard and made the tomb
secure by sealing the stone.*

Matthew 27:66

Easter
*"He has been raised from the dead,
and indeed he is going ahead of you to Galilee;
there you will see him."*

Matthew 28:7

• • •

morning + noon + night
*Over Triduum we will pause 3 times a day
for Scripture + prayer.*

• • •

• • •

HOLY THURSDAY

• • •

· ·

MORNING Matthew 26:17-30

On the first day of Unleavened Bread the disciples came to Jesus, saying, "Where do you want us to make the preparations for you to eat the Passover?" He said, "Go into the city to a certain man, and say to him, 'The Teacher says, My time is near; I will keep the Passover at your house with my disciples.'" So the disciples did as Jesus had directed them, and they prepared the Passover meal.

When it was evening, he took his place with the twelve; and while they were eating, he said, "Truly I tell you, one of you will betray me." And they became greatly distressed and began to say to him one after another, "Surely not I, Lord?" He answered, "The one who has dipped his hand into the bowl with me will betray me. The Son of Man goes as it is written of him, but woe to that one by whom the Son of Man is betrayed! It would have been better for that one not to have been born." Judas, who betrayed him, said, "Surely not I, Rabbi?" He replied, "You have said so."

While they were eating, Jesus took a loaf of bread, and after blessing it he broke it, gave it to the disciples, and said, "Take, eat; this is my body." Then he took a cup, and after giving thanks he gave it to them, saying, "Drink from it, all of you; for this is my blood of the covenant, which is poured out for many for the forgiveness of sins. I tell you, I will never again drink of this fruit of the vine until that day when I drink it new with you in my Father's kingdom."

When they had sung the hymn, they went out to the Mount of Olives.

Then Jesus went with them to a place called Gethsemane; and he said to his disciples, "Sit here while I go over there and pray." He took with him Peter and the two sons of Zebedee, and began to be grieved and agitated. Then he said to them, "I am deeply grieved, even to death; remain here, and stay awake with me." And going a little farther, he threw himself on the ground and prayed, "My Father, if it is possible, let this cup pass from me; yet not what I want but what you want." Then he came to the disciples and found them sleeping; and he said to Peter, "So, could you not stay awake with me one hour? Stay awake and pray that you may not come into the time of trial; the spirit indeed is willing, but the flesh is weak." Again he went away for the second time and prayed, "My Father, if this cannot pass unless I drink it, your will be done." Again he came and found them sleeping, for their eyes were heavy. So leaving them again, he went away and prayed for the third time, saying the same words. Then he came to the disciples and said to them, "Are you still sleeping and taking your rest? See, the hour is at hand, and the Son of Man is betrayed into the hands of sinners. Get up, let us be going. See, my betrayer is at hand."

While he was still speaking, Judas, one of the twelve, arrived; with him was a large crowd with swords and clubs, from the chief priests and the elders of the people. Now the betrayer had given them a sign, saying, "The one I will kiss is the man; arrest him." At once he came up to Jesus and said, "Greetings, Rabbi!" and kissed him. Jesus said to him, "Friend, do what you are here to do." Then they came and laid hands on Jesus and arrested him. Suddenly, one of those with Jesus put his hand on his sword, drew it, and struck the slave of the high priest, cutting off his ear. Then Jesus said to him, "Put your sword back into its place; for all who take the sword will perish by the sword. Do you think that I cannot appeal to my Father, and he will at once send me more than twelve legions of angels? But how then would the scriptures be fulfilled, which say it must happen in this way?" At that hour Jesus said to the crowds, "Have you come out with swords and clubs to arrest me as though I were a bandit? Day after day I sat in the temple teaching, and you did not arrest me. But all this has taken place, so that the scriptures of the prophets may be fulfilled." Then all the disciples deserted him and fled.

Matthew 27:11-26

Now Jesus stood before the governor; and the governor asked him, "Are you the King of the Jews?" Jesus said, "You say so." But when he was accused by the chief priests and elders, he did not answer. Then Pilate said to him, "Do you not hear how many accusations they make against you?" But he gave him no answer, not even to a single charge, so that the governor was greatly amazed.

Now at the festival the governor was accustomed to release a prisoner for the crowd, anyone whom they wanted. At that time they had a notorious prisoner, called Jesus Barabbas. So after they had gathered, Pilate said to them, "Whom do you want me to release for you, Jesus Barabbas or Jesus who is called the Messiah?" For he realized that it was out of jealousy that they had handed him over. While he was sitting on the judgment seat, his wife sent word to him, "Have nothing to do with that innocent man, for today I have suffered a great deal because of a dream about him." Now the chief priests and the elders persuaded the crowds to ask for Barabbas and to have Jesus killed. The governor again said to them, "Which of the two do you want me to release for you?" And they said, "Barabbas." Pilate said to them, "Then what should I do with Jesus who is called the Messiah?" All of them said, "Let him be crucified!" Then he asked, "Why, what evil has he done?" But they shouted all the more, "Let him be crucified!"

So when Pilate saw that he could do nothing, but rather that a riot was beginning, he took some water and washed his hands before the crowd, saying, "I am innocent of this man's blood; see to it yourselves." Then the people as a whole answered, "His blood be on us and on our children!" So he released Barabbas for them; and after flogging Jesus, he handed him over to be crucified.

LECTIO DIVINA

hosanna

What is Jesus saying or doing in this passage?

What does this passage reveal to me about God's mercy?

In what area of my life do I need to hear this message of mercy?

holy thursday

Today we begin the shortest and most intense liturgical season—the Triduum. On that Passover day 2,000 years ago, Jesus Christ instituted the highest point humanity can reach this side of heaven—the Mass—while also suffering the worst from us.

As I sit down to write this essay, it's a cold winter day. In fact, it's Christmas Eve, and I begin my meditation, as always, in front of Jesus Christ in the Blessed Sacrament.

I am stunned. Overcome. Humbled and awed by a God who knew my needs, and indeed all of our desires, so intimately. He made himself meek and vulnerable as a baby, and mocked and persecuted as a man. He did this so that we might be strengthened by his example in the difficult moments of our lives.

Yet, he also knew that a simple example wouldn't suffice. The Holy Trinity, with perfect wisdom, ordained that we might encounter perfect love, from the grandest of basilicas to the simplest of chapels, not only by hearing his holy word, but also by tasting his Body, Blood, Soul, and Divinity in the Eucharistic celebration.

God knew (and continues to know) that grace would come through encountering him spiritually and intellectually through Scripture and prayer, as well as physically in the Eucharist. He created this richness in the Mass for us, so that we could draw ever closer to him while still in exile, deep in the desert of earthly life.

The *Catechism* says:

> The Eucharist is "the source and summit of the Christian life." "The other sacraments, and indeed all ecclesiastical ministries and works of the apostolate, are bound up with the Eucharist and are oriented toward it. For in the blessed Eucharist is contained the whole spiritual good of the Church, namely Christ himself, our Pasch." (1324)

Pardon the simplicity of my response, but, wow! If that paragraph isn't a call for each of us to reorient our lives toward his presence in the Eucharist, I don't know what is.

Jesus was fully God, even while being fully man (see *Catechism*, 464), and was aware of the trials he would face. Judas betrayed him. The apostles abandoned him to sleep in the garden. Peter thrice denied him.

Jesus Christ, eternally in union with his Father and the Holy Spirit, created the Mass and gave the Eucharist to the apostles and to us, not in spite of this knowledge of our sinfulness, but because of it.

We are the unworthy children of a God who seeks us, anticipates our needs, and provides for us in abundance. He gives of himself—utterly, completely, and quite literally—regardless of our merit or lack thereof. Jesus knew that Judas would despair of his forgiveness and that Peter would repent. He knows our hearts and seeks to strengthen us with his sacraments.

This morning, before I left for Adoration, my toddler had an epic meltdown. In a moment of what I perceived to be excellent parenting, I gently and firmly redirected his behavior. I set clear limits, and doled out appropriate consequences.

In spite of my "perfect" response, he wouldn't stop crying. It wasn't until I realized it had been several hours since he last ate that I understood the important piece I had been missing. After feeding him, he was much better able to hear my commands. (So, perhaps not the pinnacle of parenting I had originally thought?)

God never intended to leave his people for millennia without feeding them. He fed the Israelites manna in the desert, he fed them loaves and fishes on the hillside, and he feeds you and me at Mass, every day if we so choose.

This terrible, awful, beautiful Holy Thursday, I invite you to reorient yourself to Jesus Christ in the Eucharist. Prayerfully consider the areas of yourself where you may have betrayed or denied Christ. Where have you rejected God's commands and therefore rejected his love? Repent of these sins, and reorient yourself towards the sanctifying grace of a spiritual and physical communion with him.

Micaela Darr

GOOD FRIDAY

Matthew 27:32-37

As they went out, they came upon a man from Cyrene named Simon; they compelled this man to carry his cross. And when they came to a place called Golgotha (which means Place of a Skull), they offered him wine to drink, mixed with gall; but when he tasted it, he would not drink it. And when they had crucified him, they divided his clothes among themselves by casting lots; then they sat down there and kept watch over him. Over his head they put the charge against him, which read, "This is Jesus, the King of the Jews."

Matthew 27:38-44

Then two bandits were crucified with him, one on his right and one on his left. Those who passed by derided him, shaking their heads and saying, "You who would destroy the temple and build it in three days, save yourself! If you are the Son of God, come down from the cross." In the same way the chief priests also, along with the scribes and elders, were mocking him, saying, "He saved others; he cannot save himself. He is the King of Israel; let him come down from the cross now, and we will believe in him. He trusts in God; let God deliver him now, if he wants to; for he said, 'I am God's Son.'" The bandits who were crucified with him also taunted him in the same way.

Matthew 27:45-50

From noon on, darkness came over the whole land until three in the afternoon. And about three o'clock Jesus cried with a loud voice, "Eli, Eli, lema sabachthani?" that is, "My God, my God, why have you forsaken me?" When some of the bystanders heard it, they said, "This man is calling for Elijah." At once one of them ran and got a sponge, filled it with sour wine, put it on a stick, and gave it to him to drink. But the others said, "Wait, let us see whether Elijah will come to save him." Then Jesus cried again with a loud voice and breathed his last.

LECTIO DIVINA

hosanna

What is Jesus saying or doing in this passage?

What does this passage reveal to me about God's mercy?

In what area of my life do I need to hear this message of mercy?

good friday

Enter into the Passion with me for just a moment. Imagine Jesus, hanging on the cross, the weight of abuse dripping off his body as he cries out to God, "My God, my God, why have you forsaken me?" (Matthew 27:47)

This verse, this cry from Jesus to his Father in heaven, kept coming back to me as I prayed through these Scripture passages. The turmoil of that moment, the utter desolation Jesus must have felt, haunts me at times. Theologians call this moment the Dereliction of Christ. The Merriam-Webster Dictionary defines dereliction as "the state of having been abandoned and become dilapidated."

Abandoned and dilapidated?

It is an apt description for what was happening in that moment of Jesus' passion. This is Christ's greatest lament. He fully embraces his humanity and completely enters into the suffering, isolation, humiliation, and complete devastation of the passion—feeling every scourge, every pound of the hammer and every thorn in his head. He hears the jeers of the crowd and endures the physical abuse heaped on him because he wants to make sure that one day you and I are standing right next to him in heaven. The more I prayed about it, the more God whispered that truth into my heart.

Jesus is showing us how to love with our whole lives in this moment. He is God, and he could have gotten down from that cross and done some damage to the people who hung him there. But instead, in a moment of supreme obedience to the Father, he remained on that cross and endured the greatest suffering that could ever be inflicted, and then he died, offering his very life because he loves you and me that much.

During the Good Friday liturgy, there is a moment when we venerate the crucifix. At our parish, we have a four-foot crucifix that the deacon holds as each member of the congregation comes forward to either touch or kiss, showing our gratitude for what Jesus has done for us. It is my favorite part of the liturgy because it brings the wounds and the suffering of Christ up close and personal.

One year, as I walked up to venerate the crucifix, I was struck by the incredible humility Jesus showed to undergo such suffering. He truly gave all he had for me. With each step I took toward that crucifix, images of Jesus undergoing great suffering kept popping into my mind, and the weight of my unworthiness to be loved in such an all-consuming way was getting heavier with each step. I don't deserve what Jesus did for me nor can I ever earn such love.

As I knelt to kiss the feet of Jesus on the crucifix, I heard in my heart, "It is my gift to you."

His gift.

Jesus gave his gift freely without expectation of any gift in return. He gave it in love, without condition. He gave it with only you in mind.

Jesus's gift on the cross is given freely, completely, and without reservation.

What is causing you pain this Good Friday? How have you been set aside or ignored? Insulted or humiliated? What difficulty or desolation are you facing right now?

Know that Jesus has already faced it and paid the price for it on the cross. The mercy and grace that poured forth from the cross on Good Friday is awesome to behold. Christ acted as the Great Physician, offering his own body to suffer and die so that we might know the depths of his love for us, offering his own lament to God in order that we may never have to utter those same words.

"Lord I am not worthy that you should enter under my roof, but only say the word and my soul shall be healed."

Thank you Jesus for the gift of your mercy, love, and redemption.

Mary Lenaburg

HOLY SATURDAY

MORNING Matthew 27:51-56

At that moment the curtain of the temple was torn in two, from top to bottom. The earth shook, and the rocks were split. The tombs also were opened, and many bodies of the saints who had fallen asleep were raised. After his resurrection they came out of the tombs and entered the holy city and appeared to many. Now when the centurion and those with him, who were keeping watch over Jesus, saw the earthquake and what took place, they were terrified and said, "Truly this man was God's Son!"

Many women were also there, looking on from a distance; they had followed Jesus from Galilee and had provided for him. Among them were Mary Magdalene, and Mary the mother of James and Joseph, and the mother of the sons of Zebedee.

NOON Matthew 27:57-61

When it was evening, there came a rich man from Arimathea, named Joseph, who was also a disciple of Jesus. He went to Pilate and asked for the body of Jesus; then Pilate ordered it to be given to him. So Joseph took the body and wrapped it in a clean linen cloth and laid it in his own new tomb, which he had hewn in the rock. He then rolled a great stone to the door of the tomb and went away. Mary Magdalene and the other Mary were there, sitting opposite the tomb.

NIGHT Matthew 27:62-66

The next day, that is, after the day of Preparation, the chief priests and the Pharisees gathered before Pilate and said, "Sir, we remember what that impostor said while he was still alive, 'After three days I will rise again.' Therefore command the tomb to be made secure until the third day; otherwise his disciples may go and steal him away, and tell the people, 'He has been raised from the dead,' and the last deception would be worse than the first." Pilate said to them, "You have a guard of soldiers; go, make it as secure as you can." So they went with the guard and made the tomb secure by sealing the stone.

LECTIO DIVINA

hosanna

What is Jesus saying or doing in this passage?

What does this passage reveal to me about God's mercy?

In what area of my life do I need to hear this message of mercy?

holy saturday

Good Friday is behind us. And today, on Holy Saturday, we sit and wait like those who were there then.

> He then rolled a great stone to the door of the tomb and went away. Mary Magdalene and the other Mary were there, sitting opposite the tomb. (Matthew 27:60-61)

This, for me, is hard to hear, because I am lousy at waiting. I start thinking of a thousand things I could be doing or should be doing or how much bother and inconvenience might come of me not doing— right now—whatever it is that I've gotten into my head. My husband (half) jokes that he has to keep a very close eye on me when we're hiking because if I were to get separated from the group, I would be incapable of following the common sense advice of staying put until someone could come back to find me. I do not like waiting.

But that's what the women of the Bible do.

> It was the day of Preparation, and the sabbath was beginning. The women who had come with him from Galilee followed, and they saw the tomb and how his body was laid. Then they returned, and prepared spices and ointments.
>
> On the sabbath they rested according to the commandment. (Luke 23:54-56)

After all of the suffering they endured on Good Friday, at the end of the day they work to prepare what they'll need to bury Christ's body. Then they wait in the stillness of Holy Saturday.

I remember being struck by this for the first time a few years ago. I was moved by how this waiting is part of God's eternal plan for our experience of the resurrection.

After all, what is Jesus doing today?

While his body lies in the tomb of Joseph of Arimathea, his spirit "descended into hell," as we say in the Apostles' Creed. To early Christians, the word "hell" as used here referred to a realm of the dead separate from that of the damned, often called the "Limbo of the Fathers," to which the souls of the righteous would go who had lived and died before Christ's atoning sacrifice on the cross. This is understood to have been a place of natural happiness rather than of suffering, but still . . . it was mostly a place of waiting.

John the Baptist had probably been chilling there for a few months, St. Joseph for a few years, Moses for over a thousand years, and Adam and Eve for many thousand years—just waiting in faithful hope that God, in his mercy, would redeem us all.

Jesus comes on Holy Saturday and reaches out to them. Their patience is rewarded.

My patience still needs work. But I do make a mindful effort, most especially on this one particular day of the liturgical year, to find time to wait in silence. I imagine myself opposite the tomb, with Mary Magdalene and Mary, the wife of Clopas. I try not to skip the waiting of Holy Saturday in my rush to head straight to the joy of Easter from the pain of Good Friday.

I love the ancient homily for today, attributed to Bishop Melito of Sardis, that reminds us,

> Something strange is happening—there is a great silence on earth today, a great silence and stillness. The whole earth keeps silence because the King is asleep. The earth trembled and is still because God has fallen asleep in the flesh and he has raised up all who have slept ever since the world began.

Of course, preparations must be made. After all, tomorrow is the greatest day of triumph and celebration of the year. People will want to eat, and these counters aren't going to tidy themselves. But even with those responsibilities, Jesus asks us to wait for him and to wait with him.

Kendra Tierney

EASTER SUNDAY

OPEN YOUR BIBLE Matthew 28:1-10

After the sabbath, as the first day of the week was dawning, Mary Magdalene and the other Mary went to see the tomb. And suddenly there was a great earthquake; for an angel of the Lord, descending from heaven, came and rolled back the stone and sat on it. His appearance was like lightning, and his clothing white as snow. For fear of him the guards shook and became like dead men. But the angel said to the women, "Do not be afraid; I know that you are looking for Jesus who was crucified. He is not here; for he has been raised, as he said. Come, see the place where he lay. Then go quickly and tell his disciples, 'He has been raised from the dead, and indeed he is going ahead of you to Galilee; there you will see him.' This is my message for you." So they left the tomb quickly with fear and great joy, and ran to tell his disciples. Suddenly Jesus met them and said, "Greetings!" And they came to him, took hold of his feet, and worshiped him. Then Jesus said to them, "Do not be afraid; go and tell my brothers to go to Galilee; there they will see me."

NOTES

182

LECTIO DIVINA

hosanna

What is Jesus saying or doing in this passage?

What does this passage reveal to me about God's mercy?

In what area of my life do I need to hear this message of mercy?

easter sunday

For all of us who profess faith in Jesus, we know well that death is not final. We have the privilege of living in the post-redemptive world in which we know that Jesus stands as victor over sin and death and that the gates of eternity have been opened for us. And yet, it still seems so final, so overwhelmingly permanent, this process of bidding the ones we love farewell for now, knowing we will not see them again this side of heaven. I am a daughter who has buried both her mother and her father. A sister who has buried her brother. A daughter-in-law who has buried her mother-in-law. A mother who has buried her baby son and said goodbye to four more little souls without ever knowing them. My life has been marked by death in profound ways. And no matter how much hope my faith gives me for a forever future with these loved ones, the goodbye here is a permanent pain that never fully abates.

Imagine, then, the grief of Jesus' friends at his death. They did not yet have the certainty of eternal life; they believed, but the good news of heaven was still buried behind a large stone. Their grief had to be great, heavy, and palpable. This was Mary Magdalene's "Rabboni," the one Peter had professed as his only place to go. And he was gone. Not only gone, but gone in a violent death of brutal torture that appeared a triumphant victory for his enemies. I can only imagine their confusion over all the talk of being the Son of Man, the glory they had seen in the transfiguration, and the promises of the life to come, suddenly seemingly nullified by this horrific death.

This is the grief the women bring with them to the tomb—the heaviness of the permanence of death. Then the earth suddenly quakes as the heavens open and an angelic presence descends, rolling back that stone that marked the end and sitting atop it pronouncing a new beginning. A simple "He is not here" upending their confused grief with the announcement of his resurrection from the dead.

They had to be flustered, confounded, and uncertain when they heard the news. And for us too, resurrection can seem confounding. We work so hard to get through the many griefs life brings our way, the loss of those we love, but also all the small deaths along the way, of hopes and dreams, of our own wills, and of futures full of hope destroyed by sin. And then we are charged, as are the women, to believe in a resurrection we cannot yet see and to bring the news of it out into the world—to be apostles of the resurrection, of the good news that death has not won.

It can be hard to assimilate it all, to at once be pained by loss and to be hopeful that God wants to redeem that loss. There are plenty of times when Pope St. John Paul's call to be an Easter person with Alleluia as my song can feel like too much to ask of my hurting heart. But Jesus, ever attuned to our human state, is not surprised that the women at the tomb are bewildered by the idea of his return from the dead. He returns to them knowing they will be afraid, overwhelmed, and confused. He lets them fall to his feet in confused relief, and he offers the gentle command to them to "not be afraid" (Matthew 28:10).

It is a jarring pronouncement that should wake us from our grief and inspire a new time of bewilderment—a confounded joy that this could be. That our human God who appeared to be utterly defeated is instead the victor. That the permanence that we feel when we face death does not have to evoke fear in us, because our God lives and whispers to our hearts, "Do not be afraid."

Whatever it is that you carried with you through this Lent—the pain you uncovered and showed to your Lord, the sin you lamented, the future you fretted over, the doubt you swirled in—you no longer have to fear it. It has been flipped end upon end and become a future full of hope, because death is overcome, and the confounding grace of the resurrection is ours.

Colleen Connell

EASTER MONDAY

OPEN YOUR BIBLE Matthew 28:16-20

Now the eleven disciples went to Galilee, to the mountain to which Jesus had directed them. When they saw him, they worshiped him; but some doubted. And Jesus came and said to them, "All authority in heaven and on earth has been given to me. Go therefore and make disciples of all nations, baptizing them in the name of the Father and of the Son and of the Holy Spirit, and teaching them to obey everything that I have commanded you. And remember, I am with you always, to the end of the age."

NOTES

LECTIO DIVINA

hosanna

What is Jesus saying or doing in this passage?

What does this passage reveal to me about God's mercy?

In what area of my life do I need to hear this message of mercy?

easter monday

"And remember, I am with you always, to the end of the age."
(Matthew 28:20)

I read these words and weep.

My father is dying. Dementia has taken hold of his once brilliant mind and has left him unable to walk and nearly unable to speak. I consider this with a little bitterness. It's been nearly two years since he's slipped from most cognizant conversation. Before that, he was an accomplished businessman and he made a living offering financial guidance to people.

I don't have a business brain. When I was in college, I traded laundry services with an accounting major so that he would balance my checkbook. My father was endlessly frustrated by the glazed expression in my eyes whenever he tried to share nuggets of business wisdom. The reality was that I really didn't need the nuggets. I was married woman, a stay-at-home mom, and the wife of a person happy to handle our finances.

All that changed two years ago, eerily coincidentally with my father's decline. I found myself a small business owner trying to learn all sorts of crucial financial skills in order to keep writing and publishing. It is an irony that after nearly five decades of having little interest in his business advice, I need it now, and he can barely speak.

A couple of months ago, troubled by all sorts of business conundrums, I went to visit him. I sat on one side of his wheelchair and my stepmother sat on the other. I told him the long story of the past few challenging months in my work world. I fought tears as I poured out frustration and disappointment and bewilderment. I didn't even know if he was awake.

He tried to lift his drooping head upright. He pulled in a bigger breath than normal. He said, "Elizabeth, don't forget…"

And then he fell asleep.

What did he want to tell me? What morsel of business wisdom did he have for me after all these years of my stubborn disinterest? And why, oh why, did I wait until it was too late? I needed his advice and he would have been so overjoyed to have shared in my new venture.

My sister and I have a rhythm in this new season of our lives. I go to see our dad, and then I call her on the way home and update her on his health, giving her a snapshot of his condition. But this time I didn't. I couldn't. I was heartbroken and I knew she'd be heartbroken, and I just had no strength to shoulder her sorrow too. So, I put off that phone call.

I put it off for several weeks.

Finally, she called me. Reluctantly, I told her the story, not wanting her to feel the sting of words we knew he wanted to say but couldn't. To my surprise she said, "I know exactly what he wanted to say."

"You do?"

"Yes, and it had absolutely nothing to do with business or financial advice or anything remotely related. He wanted to tell you the same thing he told you every night when he tucked you in, at the end of every letter, and just before goodbye in every phone call. Here, I'll fill in the gaps with you.

"Elizabeth, don't forget. Who loves you?" My sister said the words we both knew so well. How in the world, in that moment with him, did I not recognize where he was going?

"You do, Daddy," I wept, cueing the next words.

"That's right. And who else?"

"God does."

"That's right. I love you and so does God. Now go out and do life."

Love remains. Love is with us always, until the end of the age. Knowing that, we go out and do life, taking Love wherever we go and sharing it abundantly.

This is the heart of the Great Commission, to know that we are loved by Love himself and to go out and live that love.

Elizabeth Foss

**And remember,
I am with you
always,
to the end
of the age.**

MATTHEW 28:20

The End.

END DATE	PLACE

I'M FEELING

- ○ happy
- ○ excited
- ○ joyful

- ○ anxious
- ○ upset
- ○ tired

- ○ annoyed
- ○ angry
- ○ sad

- ○ grateful
- ○ confused
- ○ calm

- ○ _____
- ○ _____
- ○ _____

Scripture to share:

Three new things I
discovered about God:

1

2

3

Giving thanks for:

When did I study best?

Where did I study best?

Praying for:

What's next for my
Scripture study?

contributors

Carly Buckholz studied poetry at the University of Virginia before earning a master's degree in higher education. Often next to a pile of books, Carly spends most of her time trying to convince her friends to read more poetry and baking scones. She enjoys writing about her family, her faith, and the Blue Ridge Mountains. She currently resides in Burke, Virginia with her family.

Emily DeArdo is a central Ohio native who can often be found with tea in one hand and a book in the other (or knitting needles, or her sketchbook). She is the oldest of three children and loves rereading Jane Austen, Eucharistic Adoration, and cheering for the Pittsburgh Penguins. Along with St. Thomas Aquinas, she believes that hot baths, sleep, and good drinks (in her case, tea or Diet Coke) cure most things. She is also a wickedly competitive Trivial Pursuit player and musical theater nerd.

Colleen Connell is a bringer-upper of boys and wannabe saint who packs a little Louisiana spice with her wherever she goes. She currently serves at-risk families in her job as a social worker in Fort Wayne, Indiana, and spends copious hours on football and soccer fields yelling more loudly than all the other moms. She finds joy in the Word, the world, and the wild wonder of everyday life.

Katie Curtis grew up in Chicago but moved to the East Coast in high school and now lives in Portsmouth, New Hampshire with her giant Scottish husband and six kids (including one-year-old twin boys). A Midwest girl at heart, she loves her neighbors, coffee, and conversations that get deep. When she isn't writing or cooking she is driving her kids to sports or getting gummed on by babies. Her ideal day includes a writing session, a Rosary, a run, a dance party with her kids, and everyone home for a yummy dinner.

Micaela Darr is a California girl, born and raised, with brief stints in Mexico, Spain, and South Korea. She's extroverted by nature, but being a mom of seven kids has driven her to appreciate having quiet alone time too. Her husband, Kevin, is the best in the world, especially because he's exceedingly patient in regards to her harebrained schemes (see: living in South Korea). Micaela is disorganized by nature but is also bound and determined to improve herself in that area and has done so with a modicum of success. She loves to read, watch good TV, and chat your ear off.

Elizabeth Foss is a morning person who relishes her time alone with the Word as much as she loves the inevitable interruption by the first child to wake. There is something so hopeful about every new day! A wife, mother, and grandmother, she's happy curled up with a good book or tinkering with a turn of phrase. She alternates between giving up coffee and perfecting cold brew. Elizabeth would rather be outdoors than inside, and she especially loves long walks in the Virginia countryside that sometimes break into a run.

Kristin Foss is a self-taught artist, plant person, thrifter, minimalist-wannabe, and ENFP (who appreciates intimate gatherings). She loves a good street taco second to a loaded poke bowl, but most nights she's at home sharing a homemade dinner with her family. She gravitates towards bright, vibrant colors, and everything feminine and joyful. She believes home is a priceless place and there are no rules to your heart's idea of aesthetic and beauty.

Rebecca Frech is a big-mouthed girl who comes from a long line of opinionated women. She's a Texas girl who smokes a mean brisket and is always happy to show off her smoke rings. A self-proclaimed history nerd, she bought the house behind the town library in order to support her book-a-night reading habit. When she's not cooking, gabbing, or reading, she spends her free time raising eight children, remodeling her historic home, and sneaking off to the gym to lift all the things!

Katy Greiner thinks all mornings would be better if they started with the Dexys Midnight Runner's classic "Come On, Eileen." Her favorite way to waste time is by consuming quality long-form journalism that provokes big thoughts, and therefore good conversation. When she's not looking over her shoulder for the real adult in the room to take care of her high school freshmen, she's planning her next trip or craving Chick-fil-A. She loves a good sunset, talking over texting, tea over coffee, all kinds of music, and hearing God laugh.

Mary Haseltine is a thirty-something wife, mom, doula, and author who writes about motherhood, birth, babies, miscarriage, doulaing, marriage, faith, and any other deep thoughts that strike her fancy. She's a passionate lover of Jesus, Scripture, the Church, JPII's Theology of the Body, and her husband and six boys. When not swimming in a sea of testosterone she can be found working with doula clients, escaping from the house for a (quiet!) coffee and writing session, or enjoying a much-needed glass of wine with girlfriends. She lives in an old farmhouse in Western New York with a flock of chickens and a whole lot of dreams.

Meg Hunter-Kilmer is a hobo missionary who lives out of her car and travels around the world giving talks and retreats. In her heart, though, she lives in a house surrounded by lilacs in a small town in the South and spends her afternoons on the front porch with a stack of young adult princess books and a plate full of pastries. That not being an option, she spends much of her time making small talk, listening to audiobooks, and hunting down unlocked churches where she can make a Holy Hour. She hates bananas with a burning passion and used to keep a guitar pick in her wallet just in case—despite the fact that she doesn't play guitar.

Mary Lenaburg relishes entertaining. Her door is always open and the coffee hot. When traveling to speak, she love to explore the local candy shops looking for the perfect dark chocolate fudge (with nuts is best). Mary spends her free time reading the latest bestselling murder mystery and baking her famous chocolate chip cookies, ensuring that the kitchen cookie jar is always full. Mary and her husband have been happily married for thirty years, finding joy among the ashes since they lost their disabled daughter Courtney in 2014. They live in northern Virginia with their grown son Jonathan.

Rakhi McCormick is a wife and mother who works part-time in parish communications while trying to keep up with her husband, three young children, and a growing creative business in Metro Detroit. She is a first-generation Indian American and a convert from Hinduism. Rakhi has a passion for sharing the encouraging good news of the gospel. When not chasing her children, you can find her writing, singing, dreaming of Italy, and making beautiful things, all with coffee in hand.

Allison McGinley recently moved to the Philly suburbs with her husband and two kids and is living her dream with a church, library, and diner within walking distance. She returned to her faith during college and nothing has been the same ever since, in the best way. Writing is the way she processes life and discovers the beauty all around her, and she's been known to write in her closet in the middle of the night when the right words were suddenly found. She's happiest when taking photos of beautiful things, worshipping God through song, drinking a cup of coffee, or standing by the ocean.

Laurel Muff is a California girl who loves to travel, write, knit, read, and sing (but not necessarily in that order). She is married to her best friend and they have two beautiful girls together, whom she teaches at home. She loves to gather people around the table for delicious food and great conversation. With a heart for ministry, she is glad to share her faith in whatever capacity the Lord beckons her.

Kendra Tierney believes that anything worth doing is worth overdoing. To that end, she has nine kids (so far), wrote the book on liturgical living in the home and, in her spare time, is renovating the family's hundred-year-old Los Angeles area home. Her favorite parts are the Adam and Eve-themed laundry closet—after all, laundry *is* their fault—and the cathedral-ceilinged attic storage room that she's converted into a home chapel, complete with donated pews and stenciled ceiling, floor, and walls. She hopes to be done before the baby moves out.

Kate Wicker is a wife, mom of five, author, speaker, and a recovering perfectionist. She loves reading, running, shoes, God, and encouraging women to embrace the messiness of life instead of trying to cover it up, make excuses for it, or feeling ashamed of their brokenness or their home's sticky counters. From her home in Athens, Georgia, Kate strives every single imperfect day to strike a balance between keeping it real and keeping it joyful.

about take up & read

For nearly a decade, some friends have had a desire to write and share devotions to go along with daily Scripture study. We've traded essays back and forth in various places, and we've grown in friendship with each other and the Lord. In spring 2017, the opportunity to widen our circle presented itself. We gathered a few more women, across generations, and wrote some small essays that would inspire us—and you—to daily take up the Word and read it.

In printed journals that you can hold in your hands and touch with your pens, we collected our conversations with God. These volumes allow us to both commit at least a little time daily to honest conversation with God in his Word, and to dig more deeply and respond more carefully when we have the grace to do so. We are Catholic women who hear and pray the Word liturgically in our worship spaces and seek also to make Christ personal in our hearts and our homes. And we welcome our sisters from across denominations into our conversations at our website and on social media.

We know that the Bible is God's story for us. And we want to live in the center of that holy narrative every day. We want God's Word to give us words for one another, a common language of love in him.

God's Word endures—across the seasons of a woman's life it is the constant. He is faithful every day. In every restless night, in every joyous celebration, in all the ordinary days in between, we can and do seek the voice of our Lord in his Holy Scripture.

We take our name from the pages of St. Augustine's *Confessions*. Now a Doctor of the Church, Augustine was living a life of miserable debauchery when he was compelled by the Holy Spirit to take up his Bible and read it. His entire world changed in a moment of conversation with the Word.

We believe that ours can too—on an ordinary day, in an ordinary living room or coffee shop or college dorm, to ordinary women. We pray it is so every single day.

Our Books

Consider the Lilies

Every day of this six-week study provides Scripture to get you started and notes for further Bible reading. You will find a daily devotion, some thoughts to consider as you journal, and a prayer prompt to dovetail with your reading. Step-by-step, day by day, these words console and bring clarity to the hard days. Maybe this is a difficult season in your life—you're overwhelmed by the burdens weighing you down or the crosses that he's asked you to carry. This study is for you. It is full of the consolations of the Holy Spirit. Here, you will find a guidebook to what God is saying, how he is encouraging you to lament and to pour out your grief and your fears and your anger. Or maybe you're in a sweet spot. Life is really rather good right now. This study is for you too. It makes you a better friend to the woman next to you, to the growing child who aches, and to the spouse who despairs. And it buries words into your heart so that they are there, waiting, when the rain begins to fall. Because it will fall.

Stories of Grace

Here you will find thirty-one days of Jesus' stories carefully collected for you. Along the way, we've provided meditation essays, journaling prompts, space for your notes and drawings, beautiful calligraphy pages, and prayers to draw you deeper into the parables Jesus told. Do you have eyes to see and ears to hear Our Lord's stories of grace?

Ponder

An intimate encounter with the Rosary, this lovely volume integrates Bible study, journaling, and thoughtful daily action prompts. You will grow in your appreciation and understanding of the beautiful, traditional Rosary devotion, while deepening your love for Jesus in the gospel.

Created especially for children, this book contains Bible stories for every mystery of the Rosary. Full of interesting things to do, the journal is bursting with discussion questions, personal prayer prompts, puzzles, and coloring pages. There are also nature study pages to create a botanical rosary.

True Friend

Whether a woman is nineteen or forty-nine, friendship with other women can enrich our lives and it can make us weep. How do we find friends who are kind and true? By becoming those friends ourselves. This beautiful book invites you to explore what God has to say about lasting friendships.

Flourish

To the people of Rome, the cultural center of the world at the time, St. Paul wrote the most comprehensive expression of the gospel. For us, the book of Romans is a study of sin and guilt, of loss and rescue. It is the essential gospel. An in-depth look at the entire Letter to the Romans, this study provides inspiration and structure to dig deeply into St. Paul's guidebook for the early church—and for we who are the Church today.

Call Me Blessed

Every day of this four-week study provides Scripture to get you started and notes for further Bible reading. Step-by-step, day by day, biblical reading and inspiring essays introduce you to nineteen women of the Bible whose stories bring to life the dignity and vocation of women of God throughout the ages. Consider the stories of these biblical women in the light of the gospel and see how their truths beckon you to also become a woman of God.

bibliography

She Reads Truth Bible. Nashville: Holman Bible Publishers, 2017.

The Didache Bible: With Commentaries Based on the Catechism of the Catholic Church. San Francisco: Ignatius Press, 2015.

The Navarre Bible: New Testament Expanded Edition. New York: Scepter Press, 2008.

Augustine. *Confessions*. Translated by Henry Chadwick. Oxford: Oxford University Press, 1998.

Hahn, Scott, general editor. *Catholic Bible Dictionary*. New York: Doubleday Religion, 2009.

Hahn Scott, editor, and Curtis Mitch, compiler. *Ignatius Catholic Study Bible: New Testament*. San Francisco: Ignatius Press, 2010.

Lewis, C.S. *The Screwtape Letters*. San Francisco: HarperOne, 2015.

Kreeft, Peter. *You Can Understand The Bible: A Practical and Illuminating Guide to Each Book of the Bible*. San Francisco: Ignatius Press, 2005.

Kreeft, Peter. *Back to Virtue: Traditional Moral Wisdom for Modern Moral Confusion*. Ignatius, 1992.

---. "Part Two: Happiness: The First Three Beatitudes." www.catholiceducation.org.

2012. Accessed January 24, 2019. https://www.catholiceducation.org/en/religion-and-philosophy/philosophy/part-two-happiness-the-first-three-beatitudes.html